CRAZY HORSE
and
The Real Reason for the Battle of the Little Big Horn

Denver - Wičóni Wašté Publishing

Published by
Wicòni Wastè
P.O. Box 48005
Denver, CO 80248
Copyright © 2000
by Allen Ross

First Printing - February 2000

LIBRARY OF CONGRESS CATALOGING IN PUBLICATION DATA.

Ross, Allen
Crazy Horse and the Real Reason for the Battle of the
Little Big Horn
Bibliography: p. 108

ISBN 0-9621977-8-5

ACKNOWLEDGEMENTS

All people of the Oceti Sakowin

All Sun Dancers

My Parents: Harvey and Agnes Ross for their support.

My Wife: Dorothy Brave Eagle for her patience, understanding and love.

Proof Reader: Ben Sherman

My Typist: Lonee' Roy

Cover Artist: Janis Schmidt

My Astrologer: Mary Jayn

Artist: Marty Red Bear

My Printer: Charles Hohnstein

My children and grand children

A special thanks to my spirit guides for making this book possible.

Table of Contents

ABOUT THE COVER

In Sioux theology the number four is a sacred number. It represents the four cardinal directions, which is a symbol for Wakan Tanka (The Creator). The colors black, red, yellow and white are also sacred to the Sioux. They represent the four cardinal directions as well. Black being west, red being north, yellow being the east and white being the south.

Also in Sioux theology, the lightning is symbolic of the Wakinyan Oyate (Thunderbeings). The Thunderbeings are companions of the creator and help him do his work. In Crazy Horse's vision there appeared lightning and a horse that changed colors, these are spiritually symbolic.

The picture on the cover was chosen because of the four horses, each colored one of the four sacred colors. The horses are riderless; this represents the fact that there were no photos of Crazy Horse. Therefore no one knows what he looked like. (The figure being carved at the mountain is a composite taken from people who knew him).

This picture on the cover was painted by Janis Schmidt. Janis is a friend of my wife's family and lives in the Medicine Root District of Pine Ridge Reservation, South Dakota. This reservation is the home of the Oglala Sioux, the same tribe which Crazy Horse was a member.

DEDICATION

In the 1950's I learned of Korczak Ziolkowski's dream of carving a mountain into the figure of Crazy Horse. I was in high school on Rosebud Reservation at the time. I realized Ziolkowski was carving the mountain for us, the American Indian people. So it was my desire to volunteer to help him on the mountain. In my mind I pictured myself drilling holes in the rock, helping him, put a blasting cap with fuse into a stick of dynamite, drop it into the hole, then place a couple more dynamite sticks on top of it with the fuse coming out of the hole. This I had done while working for a miner in the Black Hills the summer of 1955. But circumstances never allowed me to assist him. Either I was busy working to earn money to go to college or I was busy with my career. In 1993 my life took a new direction. In the summer of that year, I had a book signing at Crazy Horse Mountain, which was sponsored by the book distributor, Dakota West Books. My autograph table was placed in the museum at Crazy Horse. Immediately I felt at home, I began answering tourist's questions about Crazy Horse and American Indians in general. (My doctorate work is in education with a strong minor in American Indian History/Psychology.) Thus began my relationship with the Ziolkowski family. I have since returned to Crazy Horse each summer. This work has helped me complete my desire to help

Korczak Ziolkowski's dream of carving Crazy Horse Mountain. I know I can't help up on the mountain because of my age (In a couple of months I'll be 60). But I can help by informing the public about American Indian history and culture through my books and answers to the tourist questions. (I was raised on reservations in South Dakota and have worked on reservations in Arizona, New Mexico, and North and South Dakota). Working at Crazy Horse each summer also allows me to help American Indian students. This I do by donating money to the Crazy Horse Memorial Scholarship Fund each year. It is tedious work here at the Mountain. It must be arduous for the Ziolowski family to be here 365 days of the year. To sacrifice one's own career, vacations, etc. to help people understand what has happened to the American Indians. I know because I get exhausted just being at Crazy Horse Mountain for only a couple of the months each year. To thank Ruth Ziolkowski and her family for allowing me to be a part of their effort to fulfill Korczak's dream. I am dedicating this small book to Ruth Ziolkowski.

PREFACE

In 1992 my book Mitakuye Oyasin "We are all related", won a top book award at the Frankfurt Book Fair in Germany. At that time I was the superintendent of Education on the Standing Rock Reservation, located in both North Dakota and South Dakota. Standing Rock Reservation is the home of the Hunkpapa people. It was here that I met many of the descendants of the warriors who had taken part in the Battle on the Little Big Horn River. I learned from my friend, Doug White Bull, that his Great Grandfather is the White Bull I wrote about in this book. While at Standing Rock, my wife Dorothy Brave Eagle and I self published the book Mitakuye Oyasin, so we had to do all of our own marketing and sales, etc. We soon learned that we could not sell the book as long as we were employed by the Bureau of Indian Affairs. The Bureau's Personnel Department informed us of an old obsolete law that was established back when the Indian Agents and reservation Superintendents were corrupt. At that time, the agents were usually political appointees who tried to take advantage of the local Indian populations. To counteract this practice, a law was established that BIA employees and their families were forbidden to carry on any trade or business dealings with Indians. It was called "Trading with the Indians Clause". Well, this law was still on the books, so I had to resign my position with the BIA in order to market my book. In the marketing effort to sell the book I was placed in the position to go to Crazy Horse Mountain. As a result of my book signings there, I was inspired to study about the man Crazy Horse in order to answer the tourist's questions more accurately. This interest along with the fact that I knew descendants of the people I studied made my research all the more exciting. (I am a member of the Sioux Nation and was raised on the Rosebud, Pine Ridge and Flandreau Reservations in South Dakota.) I have participated in my own culture as a pow-wow contest dancer and in spiritual ceremonialism. Having participated in the Sun Dance for 25 years and being a dream interpreter, seven years ago I was put into the position of being the organizer/leader of the Black Hills Sun Dance. I am not a holy man, nor am I a medicine man, I am just an ordinary man who has studied American Indian ceremonialism for approximately 30 years. In this book, I have used information from the spirit world to answer intriguing questions about Crazy Horse and about the Battle of the Little Big Horn. To my knowledge this is the first time this technique has been used to solve these unanswered questions. Through out this book I will use the word Sioux. It is only because when I tell the tourist my traditional tribal name, they have not heard of it. But they have heard of the name Sioux. The original seven tribes are known as Oceti Sakowin (seven campfires). Today these seven tribes

are more commonly known as Sioux. (The word Sioux is a French corruption of an Ojibwa word meaning enemy). The Individual tribes are called:
- Mdewankantonwan (Spirit Water Dwellers)
- Sissetonwan (Fish Scale Dwellers)
- Wahpetonwan (Camp Among the Leaves Dwellers)
- Wahpekute (Shoots Through the Leaves Dwellers)
- Ihanktonwan (End Dwellers)
- Ihanktonwana (Little End Dwellers)
- Tetonwan (Prairie Dwellers)

The first four tribes are known collectively as the Santee. They lived primarily on the Minnesota and Mississippi Rivers in what is now the state of Minnesota. Ihanktonwan and Ihanktonwana lived in eastern and southeastern part of what is called South Dakota today. The Tetonwan tribe has seven bands called Oglala (Scatter One's Own), Sichangu (Burnt Thigh), Miniconju (Plant by Water), Itazipco (No Bows), Ohenupa (Two Kettle), Sihasapa (Black Foot), and Hunkpapa (Camp at Entrance). These seven bands lived primarily in western North Dakota, South Dakota, Nebraska, eastern Wyoming, and in southeastern Montana. The language of the seven tribes has three different dialects. The Santee group speaks Dakota, the Ihanktonwan group speaks Nakota, and the Tetonwan speak Lakota. The original nation, the Oceti Sakowin (Seven Campfires) believed their origins were from Wicahpi Sakowin (Seven Stars of the Pleiades).

With this introduction I now invite the reader to sit back and enjoy an entirely different version of American Indian history.

AN ANNOTATED BIOGRAPHY
OF CRAZY HORSE

"All he wanted was to take care of his people and preserve their way of life".

See Appendix B

1

AN ANNOTATED BIOGRAPHY OF CRAZY HORSE

He was born in 1840, at the confluence of Cheyenne River and Rapid Creek.[1] He was born with light skin and brown curly hair. Hence his childhood name became Curly. Curly's father was named Crazy Horse. He was a Holy man, a prophet and dream interpreter. Curly had an older sister named Laughing One and a younger brother named Little Hawk.

RAISED IN BLACK HILLS AREA

Curly's mother died when he was very young.[2] His mother was a Sichangu Lakota. It was her sister that took the responsibility of raising young Curly.[3] Curly's childhood friend was named Hump. Together they learned to ride and hunt. When they reached puberty they were asked to join a hunting society called the Crow Owners. The Crow Owners were also known for their protection of the people. Crazy Horse spent most of these early years on the plains east and south of the Black Hills.[4]

---

[1] *Sources say he was born around 1840-1845 either at Bear Butte or Rapid Creek. My Spirit guides have informed me he was born in 1840 at the confluence of Cheyenne River and Rapid Creek in western South Dakota. See Appendix B*
[2] *Freedman, The Life and Death of Crazy Horse, pg.9.*
[3] *In the Lakota culture, the mother's sister is also the mother, but the mother's brother is an uncle.*
[4] *Freedman, The Life and Death of Crazy Horse, pg. 11-12, pg.49.*

FT. LARAMIE TREATY - 1851 [5]

    The Oregon Trail was established in the early 1840's. Each year immigrants using the road increased. The Sioux liked to visit these immigrants because they could receive coffee, sugar and biscuits. Traders then began to set up trading posts to trade these items to the Indians. Many traders began cheating the Indians; whiskey became a trade item, which led to more problems with the traders. In 1849 gold was discovered in California, the Holy Road became flooded with gold miners and other interested people began heading to the gold fields of California. Buffalo and other game began to flee from the Holy Road area. Favorite Sioux campsites along Platte River were destroyed because of over use. Next the white man brought cholera and small pox, which killed hundreds of Indians. Some of the warriors blamed the white man for their troubles. Raids on wagon trains and trading posts began. They increased until the white people asked the U.S. Government for protection. The result was a treaty meeting at Ft. Laramie in 1851. It was the largest gathering of plains Indians to date. Some ten thousand Indians, Sioux, Cheyenne, Crow, Shoshonis, Arapaho, Arikara, Assinaboin, Hidatsa, Mandan came to the treaty meeting. The camp was so large; horses ate all

[5] Wilson, *Wyoming Historical Tour Guide*, pg.20. *Laramie was originally two words, La Ramee, which in French means "The small branches".*

3

the grass, so they moved 30 miles east to Horse Creek. The government promised yearly goods and monetary payments for 50 years, in exchange the government wanted passage on the route west and to build forts along this route. [6] The Sioux were not to touch this road, hence it became the "Holy Road". [7] Also, the government would safeguard the right of the Indians against the whites. Crazy Horse was 11 years old and it was the first time he had seen a white man. The important thing to come out of the 1851 Treaty meeting was the government's misreading of tribal chiefs authority [8]

THE KILLING OF CONQUERING BEAR — 1854

Each spring many Sioux would return to Ft. Laramie to receive the goods/monetary payments promised in the 1851 Treaty. In the spring of 1854 Crazy Horse and his family were camped on the Holy Road (Oregon Trail) near Ft. Laramie. One day hundreds of people were gathering at Conquering Bear's camp. Crazy Horse who was 14 years old at that time, went to see what the excitement was all about. Upon arriving at the scene Crazy Horse asked an older man what was

[6] Freedman, The Life and Death of Crazy Horse. pg.21-23 The Sioux called this treaty the treaty of Horse Creek

[7] Sandoz, Crazy Horse - Strange Man of the Oglala, pg.6.

[8] McMurtry, Crazy Horse, pg.24. The chiefs authority extended only over their own immediate band.

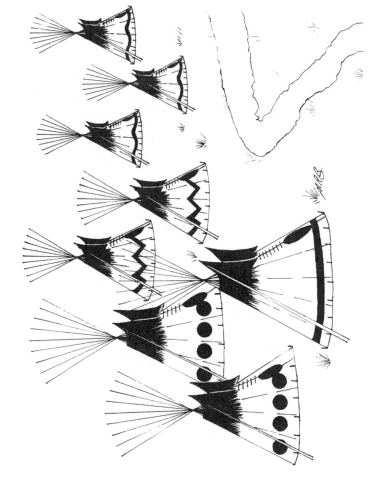

happening, the man told him that soldiers from Ft. Laramie were trying to arrest a Miniconju man for killing a lame cow. The soldiers were talking with chief Conquering Bear. But the chief told the soldiers he could not turn the man over to them because he being a Sichangu Lakota had no authority over this man. Conquering Bear then offered the man who lost the cow presents and a horse in place of the cow. The man refused saying he wanted the Miniconju arrested and put in jail. The soldiers then lined up pointed their guns at the chief and began to count. Next they began shooting. The chief fell dead. Hundreds of Sioux who were watching then attacked the soldiers and killed every one of them. [9] Later Crazy Horse learned that the soldier's leader was called Lieutenant Gratten. The soldiers killed that day numbered 32. This was the first time on the plains that soldiers were killed by Indians. [10]

[9] Freedman, *The Life and Death of Crazy Horse*, pg.28-30.
[10] McMurty, *Crazy Horse*, pg.30. *A french interpretor had been the cause of the Army's impulsive decision to open fire on Conquering Bear.*

THE VISION OF CRAZY HORSE

After witnessing this fight Crazy Horse decided to go off by himself to ponder what he had witnessed. He was 14 years old when he went out to fast, on the third day a vision came to him. A horse with a rider emerged from a body of water and began to float in the air. The horseman was dressed in breechcloth with leggings only, and wore only one feather in his hair. His hair was unbraided, and he wore no war paint. His horse pranced and changed colors as they moved closer. A voice spoke to Crazy Horse saying, "You are to help the people with what ever need they have. You are not to take anything for yourself. If you go to war, bullets and arrows will not harm you as long as you dress in plain clothes, wear your hair unbraided with only one feather on your head and carry a small stone behind your ear. Before you mount your horse you are to throw dust over yourself and your horse." A crowd of people now appeared in the vision; they tried to hold the horseman back by grabbing onto his arms. He rode through the people and kept going. A thunderstorm appeared with hail and lightning all around, the horseman kept on riding. The storm faded, showing the horseman with hail spots on his body and a zigzag streak of lightning on his cheek. In the quiet after the storm, a red tail hawk appeared over head, his scream echoing as he flew over the horseman. Now the people appeared again grabbing at the horseman's arms, but he pulled away from them and rode off. [11] The vision ended as quickly as it started. Later Crazy Horse's father interpreted the dream for him, telling him that he was the horseman in the dream. [12]

---

[11] Freedman, *The Life and Death of Crazy Horse*, pg.31-34. *The dust that Crazy Horse threw over himself and his horse was from the blind mole mound. When Crazy Horse did this it would render them invisible and invulnerable to bullets and arrows.*

[12] McMurtry, *Crazy Horse*, pg.34. *In my experience and research on dream interpretation, I learned that any dream containing water and floating are symbolic of great spirituality. In the Lakota culture lightning plays a very symbolic role, the significance being the Thunderbeings. In my book Mitakuye Oyasin pg.130-133. I found that the Thunderbeings are the same as the Christ energy. I am not a Christian per se, but I do honor concepts found in Christianity. Also in dream interpretation, when one dreams in color it is symbolic of a great and powerful dream. In Crazy Horse's vision the horses changed color, indicating the vision was in color. For clarification, dreams and visions are synonymous, one being during sleep the other while one is awake.*

BLUE WATER MASSACRE — 1855

Crazy Horse was visiting his mother's people the summer of 1855. They were camped on the Blue Water River under the leadership of Chief Little Thunder. Little Thunder was considered a friend to the whiteman so when soldiers approached he did not expect trouble. The soldiers under General Harney were seeking revenge for the Gratten affair. They surrounded Little Thunder's camp, and accused him of taking part in the Gratten killings. Little Thunder had not been at the Gratten site; he only learned of it later, so he rightfully denied having any part of the Gratten affair. Harney did not believe him and opened fire on the Sichangu camp killing 86 men, women, and children. Crazy Horse had been away from camp chasing horses with his cousin. Upon returning to camp, the sight of so much death and destruction of innocent people filled him with hatred for the soldiers. [13]

---

[13] Freedman, The Life and Death of Crazy Horse, pg38-39.

GREAT GATHERING AT BEAR BUTTE — 1857

Each year the Sioux nation would come together for a visit. The meeting of friends and relatives was always a joyous occasion. The Santee's of the east would come, Ihanktonwan and Ihanktonwana of the north and the south would come and of course the Tetonwan of the west would be there. These great gatherings were first held on the James River in eastern Dakota, later the gathering was moved to the Big Bend on the Missouri River. In 1857 it was held at Bear Butte near the Black Hills.[14] The Santee's would bring guns, metal pots, knifes, and blankets for trade. These items they received from the French of the Great Lakes. The Santee traded for buffalo hides, beaver belts, porcupine quillwork and horses. Besides being a trade fair the gathering provided the chiefs an opportunity to discuss important matters such as tribal hunting areas, white-man disease, abuse by the soldiers and of course a time to boast of their deeds. There was much dancing, Warrior society dance contests were held. The winning society would be the head warrior (Akicita) society for one year. Many social dances were also held, giving the youth time to make new friends. [15] It was at this great gathering of 1857 that Crazy Horse met the love of his

14 *Sandoz, crazy Horse, pg. 99-100.*
15 *Ross, Mitakuye Oyasin, pg.186-192.*

life. An Oglala girl named Black Buffalo Women. [16]

---

[16] *McMurtry, Crazy Horse, pg.43.*

CURLY IS GIVEN THE NAME CRAZY HORSE — 1858

Crazy Horse was now 18 years old. He was a warrior ready to prove his courage. That opportunity came that summer when his people went north and west in search of game. They came upon an Arapaho camp that had many fine horses. Crazy Horse with other Oglala youths decided to raid the camp and capture their horses. Crazy Horse prepared himself the way his vision had instructed him to do. He put a small stone behind his ear, wore a single red tail hawk feather on his unbraided hair, hail spots were painted on his body and a lightning bolt painted on his face, naked except for his breechcloth and leggings. He threw dust over himself and his horse and was ready to raid the Arapaho. The Arapaho made a strong stand and the Oglala could not break it. Suddenly Crazy Horse charged forward all by himself, he rode right through the Arapaho line counting 3 coup. [17] He then turned and galloped away as arrows and bullets flew around him but none hitting him. After reaching his own men he swung his horse around and charged again. This time two Arapaho warriors rode out to meet him, he killed them both and scalped them. Immediately he was shot in the leg by an Arapaho arrow. It was then that he

[17] *Coup is a French word meaning, "to strike". In Lakota the word is yutan, meaning, "to touch the enemy".*

remembered what his vision told him, "If you want protection, you must never take anything for yourself". He discarded the scalps and vowed never to take another scalp. [18]

Upon returning to his camp, Crazy Horse's father was so very proud of his son's deeds that he sponsored a feed and had a give away for him. At the giveaway Crazy Horse's father gave him his name Crazy Horse (until now Crazy Horse was called Curly). But now Curly had his adult name and his father became known by the name Worm. [19]

---

[18] Freedman, *The Life and Death of Crazy Horse*, pg.43-45. *In the 1600's on the East Coast, the Dutch offered a reward for dead Indians. A scalp was used as the method of collecting the reward. Indians originally only took scalps as a retaliatory measure.*
[19] *Ibid, pg.46.*

BROKEN HEART — 1864

The young Crazy Horse soon became a popular leader of the raids against neighboring tribes. He also became one of the best hunters of the tribe. Many times he would ride off hunting alone. Often he would stay gone for weeks. When he returned with game of buffalo, deer, elk and during seasonal migrations, geese and ducks. These he gave to the poor and elders. Crazy Horse was still living with his folks when he met Black Buffalo Women. He began to court her shortly after they met at the great gathering of Bear Butte. Black Buffalo Women was very popular and other suitors would come to call upon her as well as Crazy Horse. While gone for several weeks on one of his raids, Black Buffalo Women's parents arranged for her to marry Chief Red Cloud's nephew No Water. When Crazy Horse returned from the raid only to learn that his sweetheart had married someone else. It broke his heart. Black Buffalo Woman was forced to marry No Water because he came from an important and influential family. Crazy Horse felt so bad he went off by himself for several days. [20]

---

[20] *Ibid, pg.48-51.*

CHOSEN SHIRT WEARER — 1865

The Oglala had seven elders who were recognized as the band leaders. These elders belonged to the civil society, which had various names like; Owl Headdress, White Horse Owners, Big Belly, and Grey Eagle. [21] That year this society of elders decided to select four young men to be shirt wearers (Wokiconza Wicasa), whose duty was to put selfish interests aside and think only of the welfare of the people. As the selection began the first three were Young Man Afraid of his Horse, Sword, and American Horse. They were sons of important families. The fourth selection was Crazy Horse; it was a surprise because he was the son of a humble Holy man. [22]

[21] Ross, *Mitakuye Oyasin*, pg.187.
[22] McMurtry, *Crazy Horse*, pg.52-53.

HUNDRED IN THE HAND — 1866

Gold was discovered in Virginia City, Montana Territory in 1866. Soon there was a rush of whitemen trying to get there as fast as possible. The shortest route to the gold fields was straight across the Sioux reservation, even though the U.S. Government told the miners to stay out of the reservation. They crossed the reservation on a route opened by John Bozeman. The miners demanded the Army protect them as they traveled on the Bozeman Trail. General Sherman immediately started building forts along the Bozeman, while the government tried to get the Sioux to sign another treaty giving the whitemen rights to travel on and use the Bozeman Trail. [23] The treaty effort failed because the Sioux had seen how the Army was already building forts before the treaty was agreed upon. Red Cloud said to the government negotiators, "Do you think we are blind, we can see what you are doing. You treat us like children, I will talk with you no more, we will fight you for the last of our hunting grounds". Thus began the Sioux campaign against the fort builders. The Sioux leaders consulted one of the Thunder Dreamer societies, to tell them if they should attack Ft. Phil Kearny. [24] The society chosen

23 *Ibid, pg.56-57.*
24 *Freedman, The Life and Death of Crazy Horse, pg.60-67.*

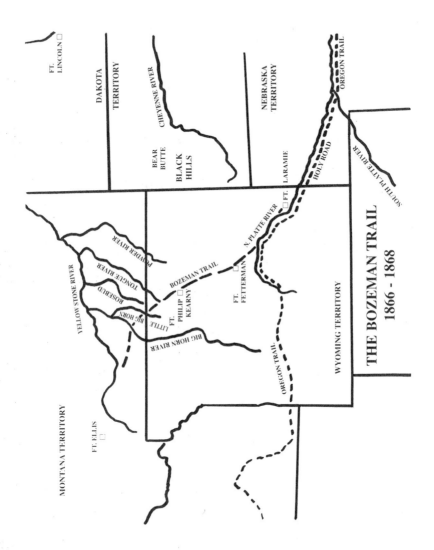

THE BOZEMAN TRAIL
1866 - 1868

to look into the future was called Winkte. [25] A renowned Winkte noted for his power of prediction rode off into the hills for a vision tooting his eagle bone whistle as he went. When he returned he held out his hands and said, "I have 100 of the enemy in my hands". The leaders shouted with approval and began to prepare to attack the fort. Ft. Phil Kearny was located in such a position that no one could approach it with out being seen. So the Sioux warrior society leaders (Akitica Itancan) decided to wait until the soldiers came out for food, water, or firewood. On a wintry day a group of woodcutters left the fort to gather firewood. The Sioux, who had now joined forces with the Cheyenne and Arapaho, sent a small force of warriors to attack the woodcutters. The bulk of their warriors waited for reinforcements that were sure to come out of the fort to rescue the woodcutters. Crazy Horse was selected to lead a group of warriors to decoy the soldiers when they came out of the fort to help the woodcutters. Captain William Fetterman was selected to lead the reinforcement troops. Captain Fetterman had boasted, "Give me a hundred troops and I'll clean out the entire Sioux

[25] *The Winkte were a society of men that dressed and acted as women. The word Win-kte when translated into English means, "to kill the woman". In psychology there exists a concept called reverse psychology. In this concept if you want a certain thing to occur you do the opposite. In order to kill the woman you allow the woman to exist, Hence Winkte. In psychological terms the woman within is known as the anima. People with these traits are thought to have the ability to connect the other side, thus providing them the power of prophecy.*

nation". As he rode out of the fort Crazy Horse appeared with 10 men and successfully decoyed Fettermen into chasing them. As Fettermen chased Crazy Horse over the hill out of sight of the fort, Crazy Horse suddenly turned his horse around and with hundreds of warriors coming out of the surrounding hills, they attacked the soldiers killing Fettermen and everyone of his troops. The Winkte's vision was fulfilled. However, the forts remained, and the fight over the Bozeman Trail soon became a stalemate. [26]

---

26 *Ibid, pg.66-70.*

IRON HORSE 1867-68

General William Tecumseh Sherman, famous for his scorched earth policy on his march to Atlanta during the U.S. Civil War, decided to do the same against the plains Indians. [27] He reasoned that as long as the plains Indians had the buffalo they couldn't be subdued. So he encouraged the railroad people to establish a railroad across the plains, often providing soldiers to help them. Once completed, the transcontinental railroad led to the killing of thousands of buffalo by trophy hunters, some of which didn't even leave the train to kill buffalo. [28] The railroad also split the great American buffalo herd into two smaller herds, the northern plains herd and the southern plains herd. [29] This two pronged effort by General Sherman sought to subdue the plains Indians, one by getting rid of their food supply and the other by forcibly establishing forts across their land. But their forts became too expensive to operate.

[27] *H.P. Howard, pg.5.*
[28] *McMurtry, Crazy Horse, pg.62-63, pg.73.*
[29] *The great American buffalo herd being split in two herds also caused some tribes that followed them to split into northern and southern groups. The Cheyenne, the Arapaho and for a time the Sioux had split. The Sichangu band of the Sioux had been following the southern herd, but eventually turned back north.*

FT. LARAMIE TREATY 1868

With the forts under siege, it became clear that the government had to make peace. The result was the Ft. Laramie Treaty of 1868; Red Cloud stated that before he signed the treaty the forts had to come down. But Red Cloud was only a warrior society chief; he was not a civil society chief. The lead civil society chief was old Man Afraid. Not until after old Man Afraid arrived and began treaty negotiations did the government agree to close the forts and reserve the Power River country as their hunting grounds. Having approved the treaty the Sioux quickly went out and burned down the abandoned forts. But the Sioux had been mislead into thinking that the boundary of their new reservation was the Missouri River on the east, Platte River on the south, the Big Horn Mountains on the west and the Yellowstone River on the North. Actually the land west of the Black Hills was reserved only for hunting trips. So the Teton Sioux unknowingly had lost their beloved Powder River hunting grounds. [30]

30 Ibid, pg.66-67.

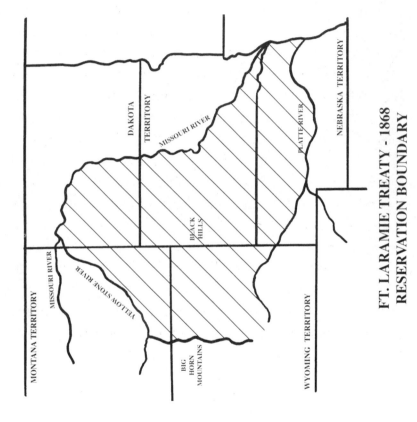

**FT. LARAMIE TREATY - 1868
RESERVATION BOUNDARY**

SHOT BY NO WATER — 1871

The Teton Sioux are descendants from an old matriarchy society. This society held the custom that a woman had the right to choose her own partner. [31] One night while her husband No Water was on a buffalo hunt, Black Buffalo Woman took her children to her parents and decided to elope with Crazy Horse. Crazy Horse was over joyed. At last he was with the love of his life. When No Water returned from the hunt and learned what had happened he took a pistol and went looking for them. Several days later he found Crazy Horse's lone tipi far from camp. He burst into the tipi shooting Crazy Horse in the face. Black Buffalo Woman ran off into the night and No Water went home leaving Crazy Horse for dead. But Crazy Horse was only wounded; the bullet had only creased his face. When healed it left a scar across Crazy Horse's cheek. When the Civil Society elders learned of Crazy Horse's actions they were appalled because Crazy Horse as a Shirtwearer had sworn to be a good example to other members of the band. After much discussion the elders decided to take away Crazy Horse's shirt. Black Buffalo

---

[31] Ross, *Keeper of the Female Medicine Bundle*, pg.226-230.

Woman was eventually persuaded to return to No Water. No Water gave Crazy Horse his best horse as a peace offering, Crazy Horse accepted with conditions that no harm come to Black Buffalo Woman. Black Buffalo Woman's next child was light skinned. [32]

Soon after the scandalous affair Crazy Horse was talked into taking a wife by his friends. He married Black Shawl Woman, and one year later they had a daughter named They Are Afraid of Her. [33]

Crazy Horse took a second wife a few years later who was half-French. Her name was Nellie Larabee aka Ella Laverie. [34]

[32] McMurtry, *Crazy Horse*, pg.69-72.
[33] Freedman, *The Life and Death of Crazy Horse*, pg.87.
[34] McMurtry, *Crazy Horse*, pg.73. *Laverie is a french word meaning a place to wash.*

A tentative genealogy of Crazy Horse

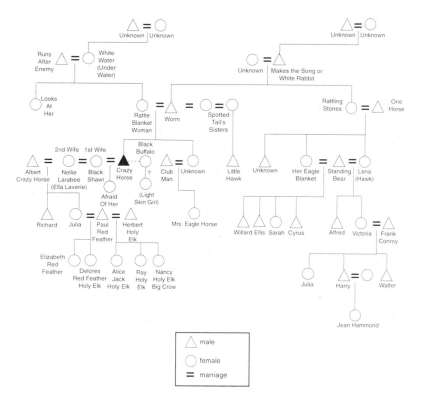

*Complete chart can be found in Appendix C.

25

FIGHT ON THE YELLOWSTONE — 1872

The Northern Pacific railroad was moving into Montana Territory from the east. The U.S. army on orders from above sent several hundred soldiers up the Yellowstone River into eastern Montana to provide protection for railroad workers. The railroad people clearly understood, that according to the Ft. Laramie Treaty of 1868, this was Sioux Country and the Sioux would not take kindly to them being there. Sitting Bull and Crazy Horse led a large war party against these soldiers. The military was well equipped, having recently received repeater rifles. Crazy Horse's attack failed to rout the soldiers,[35] but the soldiers and the railroad workers had enough. They turned around and went back east. The following spring the Northern Pacific people with an army escort commanded by George Armstrong Custer started west along the Yellowstone River again. Sioux and Cheyenne warriors decided to run off the soldiers horse herd. They caught the soldiers literally sleeping. The warriors had no intention of fighting until one of the Cheyenne recognized Custer with his long blond hair. The Cheyenne immediately turned to attack, followed by the Sioux. Custer held his own, then immediately fell back. The warriors disengaged the fight, happy to have many soldier horses. [36]

[35] Freedman, The Life and Death of Crazy Horse, pg.88-89.
[36] McMurtry, Crazy Horse, pg.76. The Cheyenne hated Custer because Custer had brutally killed Black Kettle and his people in 1868.

THIEVES ROAD — 1874

For years there were rumors of gold in the Black Hills, but the Black Hills belonged to the Sioux as verified by the Ft. Laramie Treaty of 1868. White miners began demanding the government open the Black Hills for prospecting. So General Philip Sheridan sent George Custer with an expedition of men into the hills to see if there was gold. Gold was detected and Custer sent his scout Charley Reynolds to Ft. Laramie to announce the discovery. Right away gold hungry whitemen stampeded into the Black Hills in direct violation of the Ft. Laramie Treaty. The soldiers were ordered to stop all miners from entering the reservation, but none really made any attempts to enforce the order. By the time the Sioux realized what had happened, their sacred Black Hills was swarming with greedy whitemen. Now the Sioux began to call Custer, Chief of the Thieves and his route to the Black Hills, "The Thieves Road". Crazy Horse and other leaders sent out war parties to harass the miners. The miners had heavily armed themselves and would fight to the death for this yellow metal called gold. It soon became obvious that the whiteman didn't care about the law and would not leave. The government now had to find a way to get the Black Hills away from the Sioux. [37]

[37] Freedman, *The Life and Death of Crazy Horse, pg.93-94.*

FIGHT WITH 3 STARS — 1876

The U.S. Government came up with a treaty plan to buy the Black Hills from the Indians for three million dollars. Crazy Horse's friend Little Big Man threatened to shoot anyone who signed the treaty. Crazy Horse never attended any treaty meetings himself. Someone thought he had sent Little Big Man to the meeting. The chiefs refused to sell the Black Hills. The government returned to Washington D.C. blaming the Powder River Sioux for the breakdown in negotiations.[38] President Grant met with his military advisors about the situation and a plan was formulated. The plan was to send word to the Indians living in the Powder River hunting grounds to return to their agencies by January 31, 1876 or they would be declared hostiles and the soldiers would be sent out to arrest them.[39] When the deadline passed the military sent General George Crook to round them up. He wore one star on each shoulder and one star on his hat, so the Sioux called him "Three Stars". Three Stars found a camp of friendly Indians moving to the agency. He attacked early in the morning while the temperature was 40 below zero. Most of the Indians fled up a steep hillside, rallied and counter attacked. The soldiers then made a rapid retreat up the Powder River to join General Crook's main force. The Indians

38 McMurtry, Crazy Horse, pg.82-85.
39 Freedman, The Life and Death of Crazy Horse, pg.101-102.

suffered fewer casualties than the soldiers with only two dead. But they had lost most of their possessions and food. These friendly Sioux and Cheyenne now became bitter enemies of the soldiers and they turned north to rejoin Crazy Horse. Now began the great coming together of Indian people. [40]

---

40 *Ibid, pg.103-105.*

BIG FIGHT AT GREASY GRASS — 1876 [41]

Runners were sent to the agencies asking the reservation Indians to join them. By May of 1876, half of the agency Indians had left to join the so-called hostiles. The leaders Crazy Horse, Sitting Bull, Gall, Crow King, Spotted Eagle, Touch the Clouds, along with Two Moons, Old Bear of the Cheyenne, and Inkpaduta of the Santee [42], all leaders agreed not to attack the soldiers, but if they were attacked they would then fight. The Powder River encampment grew so large, that they had to move every few days to find new grass for their horses. In June the Hunkpapa held their annual Sun Dance, Sitting Bull himself participated and received a vision. His vision showed hundreds of soldiers falling upside down into the Indian camp. On June 16, Cheyenne scouts reported Three Stars marching up from the south. Immediately an emergency council was held, the leaders decided to attack Three Stars. Crazy Horse rode at the head of 1,500 Sioux and Cheyenne warriors. They attacked at dawn, General Crooks 1,000 man force became scattered and they never could form an effective battle line. [43] As the day closed the Indians left the field, Crook having lost almost fifty men and having some

---

[41] *In the summer the grass in the Little BigHorn valley, has a shiny appearance. Hence the Lakota called the river Peji Sla Wakpa "Greasy Grass River".*
[42] *Sandoz, Crazy Horse, Strange Man of the Oglala, pg.311.*
[43] *Freedman, The Life and Death of Crazy Horse, pg.106-109.*

thirty wounded, accepted his Indian scout advice and marched back to his base camp. The Indians under Crazy Horse claimed victory. [44] The Indian encampment grew so large it had to move again. This time to Greasy Grass known to the whiteman as the Little Big Horn. The camp became two miles long and three quarters of a mile wide. It was thought to be the largest encampment of Indians ever assembled on the plains. [45] The Sioux and Cheyenne scouts had seen soldiers coming from the northwest (Colonel John Gibbon) and soldiers coming from the northeast (Colonel George Custer). The Indians felt that their camp was so large that to attack them would be fool hardy, even suicidal. So they were surprised when the shooting started on the 25th of June. Custer had sent Major Reno to attack the camp from the southeast. Reno was soon pushed back to a bluff across the Little Big Horn River. Next Custer attacked from the east. Crazy Horse, leading over 1,000 warriors, out flanked Custer from the north. Soon Custer was completely surrounded. Even though Custer had superior weapons he was shortly overrun by the Indians. Not a soul in Custer's command survived. Sitting Bull's vision was fulfilled. It was a great

[44] McMurtry, Crazy Horse, pg.94-95.
[45] Ibid, pg.84. Michno in his book Lakota Noon thought Black Kettle's village on the Washita River in 1868 was analogous to the village on the Little BigHorn River in 1876.

victory for the Sioux, Cheyenne and Arapaho. [46] Over 265 soldiers were dead and approximately 20 warriors had died. [47] That night many victory dances were held and the leaders of the Indians met in council to decide what to do next. If they attacked Reno, they could destroy him too, but it was decided to break camp and scatter in different directions. [48] This they did on the 26th of June, but not before they set the prairie on fire to hide their trail. [49] With the Custer massacre the government now had an excuse to steal the Black Hills. This they did through a treaty called the Black Hills Agreement of 1876. The required number of Sioux never signed the agreement but the government took the Black Hills in spite of the shortage of signatures. [50]

[46] Freedman, The Life and Death of Crazy Horse, pg.113-126.
[47] Michno, Lakota Noon, pg.281. Death counts were probability less, because Indian witnesses may have seen the same warrior killed. Also, the death count did not include the women and children slain by the soldiers.
[48] McMurtry, Crazy Horse, pg.105. Among the Teton, any dance associated with war is danced is a counter clock-wise motion. This represents an anti-natural movement.
[49] Freedman, The Life and Death of Crazy Horse, pg.127.
[50] Ibid, pg.130. Signed by the Sioux on Sept. 26, 1876, ratified by congress Feb. 28, 1877.

HANGING WOMAN CREEK
ESCAPE — 1877

The government wanted revenge for the Battle of Little Big Horn; they sent Colonel Nelson Miles after Sitting Bull and General Crook after Crazy Horse. Colonel Miles, called "Bear Coat" by the Indians, fought a few skirmishes with Sitting Bull, but Sitting Bull escaped to Canada as did Inkpaduta and the Santees. General Crook marched north with 2,000 men and sixty agency Sioux scouts lead by No Water. While looking for Crazy Horse, Crook came upon Dull Knife and Little Wolf camped on the Powder River. Crook attacked in a snowstorm; the Cheyenne fled, leaving all of their belongings behind. The Cheyenne went to Crazy Horse, camped on the Tongue River, for help. Crazy Horse welcomed the Cheyenne, giving them food and blankets. But with so many people to care for, Crazy Horse remembered his vision where he was to put the needs of the people first. He decided to seek peace, he sent a peace delegation to seek Colonel Miles. As they approached under a white flag, Miles' Crow scouts shot the unarmed Sioux killing five on the spot; the rest rode off to tell Crazy Horse what had happened. Crazy Horse abandoned the idea of giving up and led his people away. Colonel Miles scolded the Crow for their cowardly deed, then proceeded to follow Crazy Horse to try and arrest him. On New Years Day 1877, Miles

33

found Crazy Horse camped on Hanging Woman creek in deep snow. The soldiers attacked at dawn, but Crazy Horse held them off until the women could pack up, then the village fled to safety. The soldiers followed and attacked again, a week later the two sides fought for half a day before a blizzard stopped the battle, and Miles returned to his fort. [51]

[51] *Ibid*, *pg.131-135.*

LAYING DOWN THE GUN — 1877

Crazy Horse now realized he must surrender for the sake of his followers. In May Crazy Horse with approximately 1,000 people sat down with Lt. Philo Clark to discuss the terms of surrender. Colonel Miles wanted to claim Crazy Horse's surrender since he did most of the fighting against Crazy Horse. But in the end General Crook received all the credit for the surrender of Crazy Horse's 1,000 followers. Only 300 were warriors. After laying down his gun Crazy Horse rode into Ft. Robinson flanked by his friends He Dog and Little Big Man. They began to sing peace songs of the Lakota. Soon his warriors took up the song, then the women and old folks joined in. Thousands of agency Indians lined the route, and they began to sing also. A military officer witnessing this said, "By God, this is not a surrender, it looks more like a victory march". [52]

[52] *Ibid, pg.138-139.*

FORKED TONGUE — 1877

Many agency chiefs were jealous of Crazy Horse's popularity, especially Red Cloud, No Water's uncle. [53] But military officers flocked to meet Crazy Horse, intrigued by the fact he was never defeated in battle. [54] Soon rumors began that Crazy Horse was planning to leave the agency and returned to the warpath. These rumors had been started by No Water and his followers. The Nez Perce people were fighting against the army in the northwest and the army tried to recruit Crazy Horse as a scout to fight the Nez Perce. He refused but the army persisted. Crazy Horse told the army he came in for peace, and if they didn't leave him alone he would leave and go north. The interpreters began arguing over what Crazy Horse meant. Scout Frank Forward said Crazy Horse meant to return to the warpath. Scout Bill Garnett said Crazy Horse only wanted to go north to hunt buffalo, as promised when he surrendered. With so much confusion going on about what Crazy Horse actually said, No Water's followers quickly ran to General Crook and told him Crazy Horse was plotting to kill him. Crook ordered Crazy Horse to be brought in by the Indian police which were under the leadership of No Water. [55] Crazy Horse

[53] *Ibid, pg.141-142.*
[54] *Ibid, pg.140*
[55] *Ibid, pg.142-144.*

fled to his uncle's camp, the Sichangu chief Spotted Tail. Upon arriving he told his uncle the truth, he had done nothing to violate the terms of his surrender. Spotted Tail agreed to go with Crazy Horse to Ft. Robinson, so that Crazy Horse's side of the story could be heard. Upon returning to Ft. Robinson, Lt.Lee from the Spotted Tail agency, who had been riding with Crazy Horse and Spotted Tail, went straight to the post commanders office and asked to see Lt.Colonel Bradley. But Bradley, having orders from General Crook to arrest Crazy Horse, sent four Indian policemen to bring him in. Crazy Horse thought he was being escorted to see Bradley. Soon he realized he was being taken to the Guard House. Jerking free, he pulled a small knife but Crazy Horse's friend Little Big Man, who was now an Indian police, grabbed Crazy Horse from behind pinning his arms to his side. [56] A soldier guarding the Guard House stepped forward and bayoneted Crazy Horse in the back. [57] Crazy Horse died in the early morning of September 6, 1877. [58] During his life he had lost his brother Little Hawk, his beloved daughter Afraid of Her, the love of his life Black Buffalo Woman,

[56] *Clark, The Killing of Chief Crazy Horse, pg.33-36.*
[57] *Ibid, pg.143. The soldier that killed Crazy Horse was named William Gentles. After the bayoneting of Crazy Horse, the army quickly sneaked him out to Camp Sidney for his own safety. Gentles died mysteriously seven months later; cause of death was listed as asthma.*
[58] *McMurtry, Crazy Horse, pg. 139. Also, Indian sources say Crazy Horse died in the early morning of Sept. 6th, 1877.*

his friends Hump and Lone Bear, his way of life, and many Oglala who didn't understand him. Now he had lost his life. [59] Crazy Horse's elderly parents took his body north toward the Badlands. The next day they returned without his body. (A short time later, Crazy Horse's wife Black Shawl, who was sick with tuberculosis, died.) His parents never revealed the location of Crazy Horse's burial, leaving his memory to remain an enigma to this day. [60]

HO HECETU YELO
"That's the way it is"

"Shortly before crazy Horse was arrested at Ft. Robinson, he had a premonition that he would be killed. So he told his followers if this should happen, 'Paint my body red and dip me in spring water and I'll come back to life. If you don't, then I'll turn to stone.' During the confusion and turmoil of his death, his followers forgot to paint him red and put him in spring water." [61] Many people feel the carving of Crazy Horse mountain is the fulfillment of his prophecy.

---

[59] McMurtry, Crazy Horse, pg.133.
[60] Clark, The Killing of Chief Crazy Horse, pg.36.
[61] Kadlecek, To Kill an Eagle, pg. 49.

FIGHT ON THE GREASY GRASS
(Battle of the Little Big Horn)

FIGHT ON THE GREASY GRASS
(Battle of the Little Big Horn based on the oral history of the Sioux, Cheyenne and Arapaho)

In the summer of 1876, the army had orders to round up the so-called hostiles living in the Powder River hunting grounds and bring them back to the reservation. The army initiated a three pronged campaign; Colonel John Gibbon marched east from Ft. Ellis in Montana Territory. General Alfred Terry marched west from Ft. Lincoln in Dakota Territory; General George Crook marched north from Ft. Fettermen in Wyoming Territory. These three armies totaling nearly 3,000 men planned to meet in the Little Big Horn River country by late June. [1] General Terry was the first to reach the Little Big Horn area. Scout's reported lots of Indians on the Rosebud River. Terry dispatched Colonel George Custer and the 7th Cavalry to march south along the Rosebud, cut west to the Little Big Horn River, turn back north and rejoin Terry and Gibbon on the Yellowstone River. The plan was to catch the Indians from two sides. But first they had to find them. Custer was traveling lightly, taking only his cavalry and pack mules so he could travel fast. He knew from previous experience that if he wanted to catch Indians he

[1] *Hardoff, Lakota Recollections of the Custer Fight, pg.10-11.*

had to travel fast. [2] On the eve of June 24th, Custer's scouts found a huge Indian trail. Custer marched all night hoping to catch up with the Indians. Early in the morning Custer's Indian scouts confirmed a large village in the valley of the Little Big Horn. His regiment was sighted by several Indian parties, so now surprise was no longer on his side. He had to move fast he thought, if he was to make a fight of it. General Terry's instructions to Custer were do not let the Indians escape to the south. [3] Custer sent Captain Frederick Benteen with three companies to the south to cover any southerly escape the Indians may try. Custer then sent Major Marcus Reno with three companies to the west and north along the Little Big Horn River to attack the village from the south. Colonel Custer with five companies then headed northwest along the bluffs on the northeast side of the Little Big Horn. [4] Custer's Indian scouts had reported the presence of a huge encampment along with their enormous herd of horses. [5] Either he didn't believe the scouts or thought he could defeat them anyway. When Custer reached the top of Medicine Tail Coulee a scout reported to him that Major Reno had already attacked the village and was being

[2] *Henckel, The Battle of the Little Big Horn, pg.10-12.*

[3] *Hardoff, Lakota Recollections of the Custer Fight, pg.12-13.*

[4] *Henckel, The Battle of the Little Big Horn, pg.16.*

[5] *Michno, Lakota Noon, pg.59. The horse herd was estimated to be between 20,000 to 25,000. My spirit guides have informed me that there was 22,000 horses in the herd.*

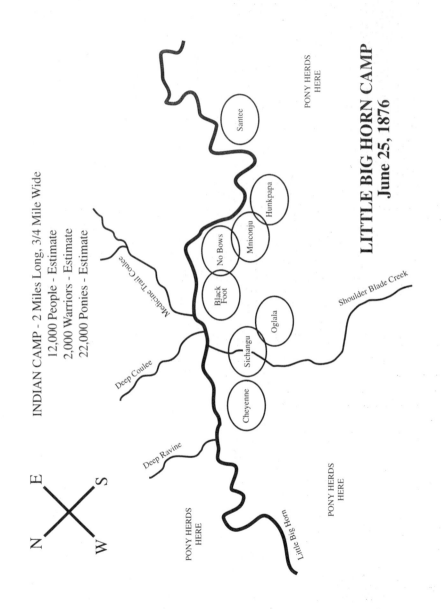

INDIAN CAMP - 2 Miles Long, 3/4 Mile Wide
12,000 People - Estimate
2,000 Warriors - Estimate
22,000 Ponies - Estimate

LITTLE BIG HORN CAMP
June 25, 1876

PONY HERDS HERE

Santee

Hunkpapa

Mniconju

No Bows

Black Foot

Oglala

Sichangu

Cheyenne

Medicine Trail Coulee

Shoulder Blade Creek

Deep Coulee

Deep Ravine

Little Big Horn

PONY HERDS HERE

PONY HERDS HERE

N E S W

driven back. At this point Custer still could not see the tremendous size of the village. He sent Captain Myles Keogh with three companies toward Calhoun Hill. Custer with Captain George Yates and two companies went down Medicine Tail Coulee toward the river. He hoped that his presence in this area would draw pressure off Reno. Reno had crossed to the west side of the Little Big Horn River and started north along the river. Major Reno then attacked the village. [6]

It was about mid-morning when the attack started according to Indian sources. [7] The cry went out "the chargers are coming, the chargers are coming". Black Elk could hear the alarm being given from one camp to the next. Low Dog heard the alarm but did not believe it, because the village was so large no whiteman would dare to attack. [8] The first to face the soldiers attack were the Santee. They were camped among the trees along the river at the most southern part of the village. Inkpaduta and White Lodge, leaders of the Santee, immediately began calling their men to fall back into the woods. Inkpaduta was 60 years old and had been fighting whitemen since 1857. He knew instinctively what to do. He wanted his men to wait until the soldiers passed, and then they would come out of hiding

[6] *Ibid, pg.106-108. My spirit guides provided the location for each tribe with the Little Big Horn camp.*
[7] *Hardoff, Lakota Recollections of the Custer Fight, pg.39-40. Official army investigation put the beginning of the battle at 1:00 far western time. For length of battle, see Appendix D.*
[8] *Michno, Lakota Noon, pg.24-25.*

from behind and attack to the rear of the soldiers. [9] White Bull said he was watering his horses at mid-morning when he heard the alarm. He climbed a small hill and could see the soldiers coming. He jumped on his horse and chased his herd back to camp. [10] Antelope said it was beginning to be another hot day, so she and her friends went to the river to swim. Antelope was a Cheyenne, so when two Lakota boys came running sounding the alarm, "The chargers are coming", she did not understand them, but instinctively knew something terrible was approaching. [11] By this time, Major Reno's advance had reached the edge of the Hunkpapa camp, they began shooting at anybody, men, women and children. [12] Gall, a Hunkpapa leader, was sitting in his tipi when the alarm, "The chargers are coming", sounded. He immediately started north to get his horse. When he returned, his two wives and three children lay dead from the soldier's bullets. [13] Beard, also known as Iron Hail, was a Miniconju. His people were led by Hump, Fast Bull and High Back Bone. He said that Crazy Horse led the Oglala, Inkpaduta led the Santee, and Lame Whiteman led the Cheyenne. When they camped together they all looked to Sitting Bull as their leader. [14]

[9] Van Nuys, Inkpaduta - The Scarlet Point, pg.396-401.
[10] Michno, Lakota Noon, pg.25-26.
[11] Ibid, pg.24.
[12] Ibid, pg.51.
[13] Ibid, pg.38, pg.155
[14] Ibid, pg.29.

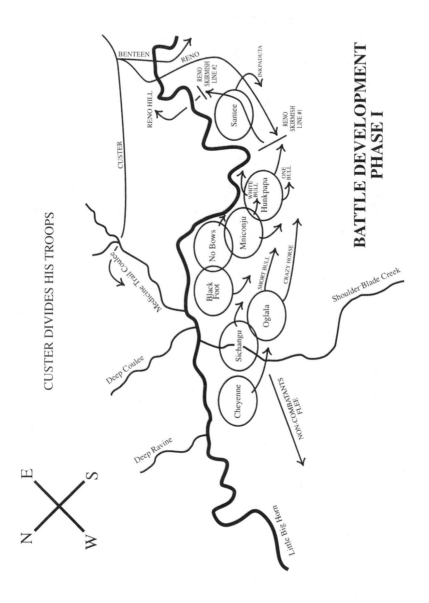

CUSTER DIVIDES HIS TROOPS

BATTLE DEVELOPMENT PHASE I

One Bull ran to his uncle Sitting Bull's tipi to learn what he should do. Sitting Bull gave him his shield and told him to go out and meet the soldiers. Hold up my shield, tell them I would like to talk peace. But Sitting Bull was only stalling for time; his main concern was to get the women and children to safety. [15] When Major Reno reached the edge of Sitting Bull's Hunkpapa village, warriors started appearing from everywhere. Reno called to form a skirmish line. Old Indian men and women were now singing songs of encouragement to the warriors. The songs excited the warriors to rally against the soldiers. Reno's skirmish line began to bunch. [16] He was quickly becoming panicky, just then Bloody Knife, a scout riding beside Reno was shot in the head, spattering matter and blood all over Reno. The shaken Reno immediately called for a retreat. [17] As Reno turned he ran into Inkpaduta's Santee. Inkpaduta's ambush worked. [18] Reno temporarily formed a second skirmish line only to retreat in bloody panic across the Little Big Horn River. [19] In the mean time Arikara scouts were busy stealing Sioux horses. Many Sioux had seen what the Arikara were doing and charged the scouts. The Arikara wisely left their stolen horses and headed

15 *Ibid, pg.39.*
16 *Ibid, pg.56-59.*
17 *Ibid, pg.87.*
18 *Van Nuys, Inkpaduta - The Scarlet Point, pg.401.*
19 *Michno, Lakota Noon, pg.87-89.*

back east. [20] Red Hawk said the Indians chased Reno across the river, many soldiers were on foot. They killed about forty soldiers as they fled to the top of a bluff. Here they corralled them into a small place. [21] Red Feather said he got a late start in the fight against Reno because he had been out all night with the girls. By the time he caught his horse and went to fight, Reno had already formed a line of soldiers. Red Feather said as we charged them, the soldiers took down their flags and retreated to the woods behind them. After a short while the soldiers rushed out of the woods only to meet Crazy Horse and his men. The Indians chased the soldiers across the river and up the bluffs. Red Feather said only ten men made it up the bluff and made a defense. Suddenly the women and children began shouting there are more soldiers on the north. Crazy Horse and the Oglala's left immediately for the north side of the camp. When they arrived, the Cheyenne were already fighting Custer and his men. We Oglala acted as rein-forcements. We charged the soldiers twice, Red Feather said on the second charge I had my horse shot out from under me. [22] Gall had seen Crazy Horse, with a great many men, race to the north to attack Custer. [23] Short Bull who had been fighting Reno talked with Crazy

20 *Ibid, pg.57.*
21 *Hardorff, Lakota Recollections of the Custer Fight, pg.40-41.*
22 *Ibid, pg.81-85.*
23 *Michno, Lakota Noon, pg.68.*

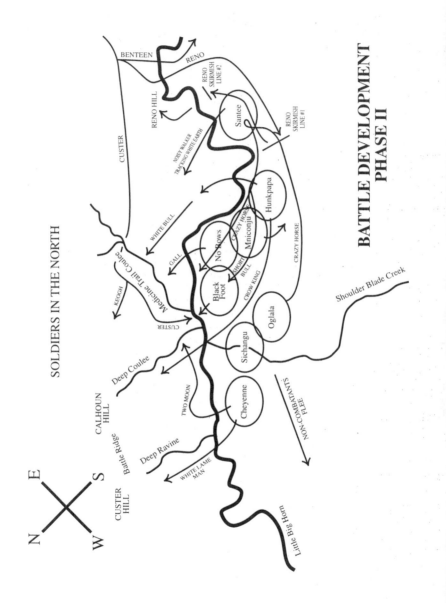

SOLDIERS IN THE NORTH

BATTLE DEVELOPMENT
PHASE II

BENTEEN

RENO

RENO HILL

CUSTER

RENO
SKIRMISH
LINE #2

RENO
SKIRMISH
LINE #1

Santee

NOISY WALKER
TRACKING WHITE EARTH

Hunkpapa

WHITE BULL

No Bows

CRAZY HORSE

Mniconjú

GALL

SHORT
BULL

CROW KING

CRAZY HORSE

KEOGH

Black
Foot

Medicine Trail Coulee

CUSTER

Oglala

Shoulder Blade Creek

Deep Coulee

Sichangu

CALHOUN
HILL

TWO MOON

NON-COMBATANTS
FLEE

Battle Ridge

Cheyenne

Deep Ravine

CUSTER
HILL

WHITE LAME
MAN

Little Big Horn

N E S W

48

Horse just before they left to go north, Crazy Horse told him, "There is a great fight coming over the hill," then both men turned and led their followers north. [24] Crow King followed behind Crazy Horse with many more men. [25] Gall stated as he left the Reno fight Inkpaduta's twin sons, Noisy Walker and Tracking White Earth accompanied him toward the north. All three men joined Crow King and went after Custer. [26] After Custer had sent Captain Keogh to Calhoun Hill he and Captain Yates went down Medicine Tail Coulee to cross the river. [27] Hollow Horn Bear said as the soldiers came toward the river, it appeared that they were hesitant to cross the river. [28] White Cow Bull said the soldiers did attempt to cross the river, but he and several other warriors began shooting at them. One of the shots hit a man dressed in buckskin in the chest. He fell from his horse; two soldiers rode along side and picked him up. The soldiers then turned and started up to the top of Custer Hill. [29] Now all of Custer's men held an elevated position. Keogh on top of Calhoun Hill and Custer on top of Custer Hill. Hump says that Custer went north and west, it appeared they wanted to cover any retreat. [30]

[24] *Ibid, pg.97-98.*
[25] *Ibid, pg.177-178.*
[26] *Van Nuys, Inkpaduta - The Scarlet Point, pg.402.*
[27] *Taken from the video, Custer's Last Battle, with Richard A. Fox. PhD.*
[28] *Michno, Lakota Noon, pg.131.*
[29] *Ibid, pg.119. My spirit guides informed me that the man dressed in buckskin was George A. Custer.*
[30] *Ibid, pg.132.*

Fox thought Custer went to try and cover the retreat of the non-combatants. When he realized there were too many of them he turned and then went on top of Custer Hill. [31] Wolf Tooth stated that the Cheyenne were the first to meet the soldiers at the river. [32] When the Sioux reinforcements arrived, together they attacked the soldiers and pushed them up the hill stated Ice. [33] Custer's five companies now held the high ground, a military advantage. But the Indians quickly started to flank the soldiers and then began to encircle them. On our first attack up Calhoun Hill we were forced back, too many soldiers, I counted four companies, White Bull declared. [34] Flying Hawk rode with Crazy Horse as they worked their way north to a place at the rear of the soldiers. [35] Two Moon circled around the northwest side of the soldiers, [36] with Crow King in front and Crazy Horse behind the soldiers, they were now completely surrounded. Two Moon attacked but had to fall back. [37] Next Crow King attacked and began to advance steadily. Many Blue Coats still on their horses suddenly dismounted, so we spooked their horses, said Crow King. Wooden Leg saw many soldiers ride toward Custer Hill

[31] *Taken from the video, Custer's Last Battle, with Richard A. Fox Ph.D.*
[32] *Michno, Lakota Noon, pg.137.*
[33] *Ibid, pg.132.*
[34] *Ibid, pg.163.*
[35] *Ibid, pg.165.*
[36] *Ibid, pg.166.*
[37] *Ibid, pg.173-174.*

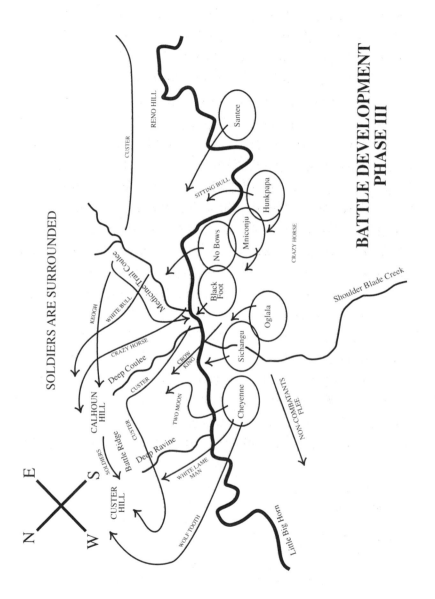

BATTLE DEVELOPMENT
PHASE III

SOLDIERS ARE SURROUNDED

RENO HILL

CUSTER

Santee

SITTING BULL

Hunkpapa

Mniconju

No Bows

CRAZY HORSE

Black Foot

Oglala

Sichangu

Shoulder Blade Creek

KEOGH

WHITE BULL

Medicine Trail Coulee

CRAZY HORSE

Deep Coulee

CUSTER

CROW KING

CALHOUN HILL

CUSTER

TWO MOON

Cheyenne

NON-COMBATANTS FLEE

Battle Ridge

CUSTER

Deep Ravine

WHITE LAME MAN

SOLDIERS

CUSTER HILL

WOLF TOOTH

Little Big Horn

N
E
S
W

51

then dismount. The Indians fell back briefly then Lame Whiteman rallied the warriors for an attack. [38] Wolf Tooth spoke of how criers told all Indians to wait for the attack by the Dead Dance boys, and then they were to rush in behind them. As they attacked with many warriors it became hand to hand fighting. Lame Whiteman rode through the soldiers but was killed on the other side, said Wolf Tooth. [39] Meanwhile on Calhoun Hill, Crazy Horse and White Bull led a similar charge counting many coups as the Sioux swarmed over the Blue Coats. White Bull had his horse shot out from under him. He got up to walk when he noticed he was shot in the leg. [40] The attacks on both hills marked the beginning of a rapid deterioration of Custer's defensive line. He Dog noticed soldiers leaving both hills and running for the river. [41] Two Eagles said he saw about 12 soldiers run toward the river and jump into deep ravines. [42] After the battle the burial party found 28 dead soldiers in a deep ravine. The Last Stand was in the ravine, not on top of Custer Hill. [43] That night at the victory dance, the Santee Noisy Walker proudly showed everyone his

---

[38] *Ibid, pg.177-178, pg.196-197.*
[39] *Ibid, pg.197, pg.204.*
[40] *Hardorff, Lakota Recollections of the Custer Fight, pg.115-116.*
[41] *Michno, Lakota Noon, pg.219.*
[42] *Hardorff, Lakota Recollections of the Custer Fight, pg.146.*
[43] *Ibid, pg.32. In the footnote, respects nothing states the battle ended in the ravine, also my spirit guides informed me that the Last Stand was at the deep ravine.*

prize. It was Custer's Horse. [44] The next day the besieged Reno was surprised when the Indians packed up and left the valley. They headed west for the Big Horn Mountains. As they left, the prairie was set on fire behind them, hiding their escape route and destroying food for any of the soldier's horses that might follow them. [45]

[44] Michno, Lakota Noon, pg.290.
[45] Henckel, The Battle of the Little Big Horn, pg.29.

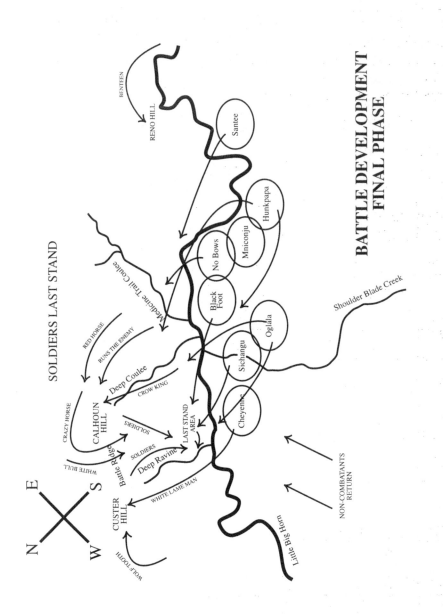

BATTLE DEVELOPMENT
FINAL PHASE

SOLDIERS LAST STAND

Santee

Hunkpapa

Mniconju

No Bows

Black Foot

Oglala

Sichangu

Cheyenne

Shoulder Blade Creek

BENTEEN

RENO HILL

Medicine Trail Coulee

RED HORSE

RUNS THE ENEMY

Deep Coulee

CROW KING

CRAZY HORSE

CALHOUN HILL

SOLDIERS

Battle Ridge

SOLDIERS

WHITE BULL

LAST STAND AREA

Deep Ravine

WHITE LAME MAN

CUSTER HILL

WOLF TOOTH

NON-COMBATANTS RETURN

Little Big Horn

N E
  S W

54

ORAL HISTORY WAS BY THE FOLLOWING MEN AND THEIR TRIBAL AFFILIATION

CHEYENNE
ANTELOPE
LAME WHITEMAN
ICE
WOLF TOOTH
TWO MOON
WOODEN LEG

MINICONJU (SIOUX)
BEARD
HUMP
FAST BULL
HIGH BACK BONE

OGLALA (SIOUX)
BLACK ELK
CRAZY HORSE
RED HAWK
RED FEATHER
WHITE COW BULL
FLYING HAWK
HE DOG
SHORT BULL

ARAPAHO
WATERMAN

SANTEE (SIOUX)
INKPADUTA
NOISY WALKING
TRACKING WHITE EARTH
WHITE LODGE

HUNKPAPA (SIOUX)
WHITE BULL
GALL
SITTING BULL
ONE BULL
CROW KING

SICHANGU (SIOUX)
HOLLOW HORN BEAR
TWO EAGLE

ARIKARA
BLOODY KNIFE

THE REAL REASON FOR THE BATTLE OF
THE LITTLE BIG HORN

THE REAL REASON FOR THE BATTLE OF THE LITTLE BIG HORN
(An Inquiry)

While reading information about the Federal Reserve System all of a sudden it dawned on me that it was the manipulation of the "medium of exchange" that caused the Battle of the Little Big Horn. Let me explain:

POLARIZATION OF THE WEALTH

In the summer of 1990 at the Sun Dance, I told the participants there the reason I planned to pull seven buffalo skulls. I wanted the spirits to help me find out why there was so much alcoholism on the reservation. The story about alcoholism I told was about a car accident that I had witnessed earlier that summer as I was coming back from Rapid City, heading toward the reservation, when a car went around us doing about 90 mph. I noticed it was people from the reservation who appeared to be drinking. We got about three miles down the road and found their car in the ditch. They had wrecked. It was a terrible accident! We stopped; I ran down to the car; the dust was just settling. The two people in the car were completely mangled. The boy had part of his face gone, his chest was crushed and his legs were all mangled. The girl's head from her forehead back had been gashed open and it looked like she had been scalped. It was terrible! A man with a car phone arrived and called the police. As we waited for the police and ambulance, I remembered how helpless I felt about this situation. I picked four sprigs of sage and said a prayer for the victims. All of a sudden, a force came around the boy, whirling above him for about a minute, then lifting up and disappearing. I believe it was the spirits who had come to receive the boy's spirit into the spirit world. Shortly after this, the ambulance arrived and took the two to the hospital.

As a result of witnessing this accident, I felt that drinking is just a symptom of something deeper that is happening to our Lakota people. I feel that it's not really the people's fault what is happening to them. Therefore I pulled the buffalo skulls to learn why alcohol is affecting 100% of the People on the reservations. Even if one doesn't drink, someone in one's family does. [1]

During the past few months, I had read The Phoenix Journals referred to earlier. In going through them, I came across information about the Federal Reserve System. The Journals explain that the reason America is in the economic condition it is today is because of the Federal Reserve System, which is not a

---

[1] *Ross, Ehanamani - Walk Among, pg.173. To pull buffalo skulls, one must pierce a wooden skewer through the skin on the back. Then fasten a rope which had been tied to the skulls, one then drags the skulls until the skin breaks.*

government entity, as some people believe. [2] The Phoenix Journals also point out that the Federal Reserve has never been audited. It is controlled by a private banking cartel that works as follows: the U.S. Treasury prints money and the Federal Reserve buys it - two cents on the bill, regardless of denomination - then turns around and lends this money and charges interest. The Journals also state that the Federal Reserve controls the economy of this country. Unfair capitalism?

Material from the Phoenix Journals about the Federal Reserve just came to me. Did the spirits give me an answer to my question: Why is there so much poverty and alcoholism on the reservations?

The Phoenix Journals were written by automatic writing, now many modern people don't believe in automatic writing; therefore, I needed to find evidence from research to substantiate what I had discovered about the Federal Reserve System. Once again, I relied on synchronicity to provide the findings I needed to read.

In doing a show in Pasadena, California, I had made a comment to one of the people visiting my booth about the Federal Reserve System. A woman standing there agreed with what I had said. As we began to talk about the Federal Reserve, she said that she had a small library of books that she could share with me so I could

[2] *Ibid, pg.206. Economic condition in America means a polarization of the wealth.*

become more familiar about the Federal Reserve System.

As I read the book, Billions for the Bankers, Debts for the People by Sheldon Emry, I was able to understand how the Federal Reserve System affected our lives on Indian reservations. To illustrate what Emry speaks about: when the U.S. Government established its budget, let's say that they had a spending budget of one billion 500 million dollars. They then subtract from this amount their income acquired from taxes and assets. Now let's say that their income was one billion dollars. This would leave a deficit of 500 million dollars. The U.S. budget is created for U.S. Government expenditures. Examples: armed forces, government employees, federal aid to states, and poverty programs. Well, Uncle Sam, the U.S. Government, says to the Federal Reserve System, "I need 500 million dollars to pay the deficit".

The Federal Reserve responds by saying, "We will print the money and then lend it to you in return for interest-bearing U.S. bonds". Congress then authorizes the Treasury Department to print the bonds for the Federal Reserve. The Federal Reserve, in turn, pays the cost of printing money for the government. The U.S. bonds are held as reserves to create credit for additional loans. How does this affect the people on the reservation? In some cases, 80% of the people on reservations are unemployed. Extreme poverty exists on reser-

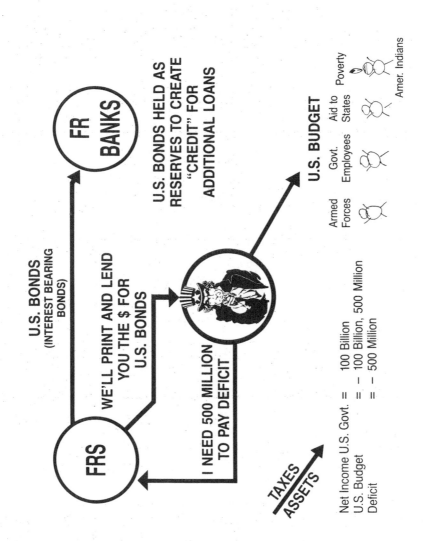

U.S. BONDS
(INTEREST BEARING BONDS)

FR BANKS

U.S. BONDS HELD AS
RESERVES TO CREATE
"CREDIT" FOR
ADDITIONAL LOANS

FRS

WE'LL PRINT AND LEND
YOU THE $ FOR
U.S. BONDS

I NEED 500 MILLION
TO PAY DEFICIT

TAXES
ASSETS

U.S. BUDGET

Armed Forces   Govt. Employees   Aid to States   Poverty

Amer. Indians

Net Income U.S. Govt. = 100 Billion
U.S. Budget = – 100 Billion, 500 Million
Deficit = – 500 Million

61

vations. The U.S. Government rejoins by sending welfare program dollars to the reservations and, as a result, keeps the reservations on welfare mentality. Reservation residents cannot get loans from the banks because the banks won't loan without collateral. The land on reservations is held in trust by the U.S. Government. Therefore, the banks won't lend money to individuals whose land is held in trust.

Thus, it becomes a "catch 22" situation and the people on the reservations are continually held in a state of poverty and welfare.

The only exception is that some tribal councils are able to get loans from banks (which are members of the Federal Deposit Insurance Corporation) on collateral of tribal land. How can this be possible when the land is held in trust by the U.S. Government? (Is the Bureau of Indian Affiars playing politics again?) Some tribes are on the verge of receivership. Who will get the land if a tribe goes into receivership? The banks or the Federal Reserve System? How can land held in trust by the U.S. Government be turned over to a "private bank"? Only Congress has the power to do that. Who does, indeed, control Congress? The people or special monetary lobbyists?

I shared this observation with a white acquaintance who said he had had guilt feelings about what has happened to the American Indians. After I explained the Federal Reserve System to him, he said he no longer felt guilty when he realized it is the bankers that control the Federal Reserve System who are to blame, not only for poverty on the reservations, but for poverty that exists throughout this country.

In the Secrets of the Federal Reserve by Eustace Mullins, the author was asked:

When Congress passed the Federal Reserve Act on December 23, 1913, did the Congressmen know they were creating a central bank? Answer - members of the 63rd Congress had no knowledge of a central bank or of its monopolistic operations. Many of those who voted for the bill were duped, others were bribed, and others were intimidated. The preface to the Federal Reserve Act reads, 'An act provided for the establishment of the Federal Reserve banks to furnish an elastic currency to afford means of rediscounting commercial papers to establish a more effective supervision of banking in the United States and for other purposes'. The unspecified other purposes were to give international conspirators a monopoly of all the money and credit of the people of the United States. To finance World War I through the new central bank to place American workers at the mercy of the Federal Reserve's collection agency, the Internal Revenue Services, and to allow the monopolists to seize the assets of the competitors and put them out of business.

Mullins goes on to say "the dynastic families of the ruling order are internationalists who are loyal to no race, religion or nation. They are the people who own the stock of the Federal Reserve banks".

Mr. Mullins was further questioned about anyone being able to buy this stock. He replied, "No, the Federal Reserve Act stipulates that the stock of the Federal Reserve banks cannot be bought or sold at any stock or exchange. It is passed on by inheritance as a fortune of the big rich. Almost half of the owners of the Federal Reserve banks' stock are not Americans."

Another question asked of Mr. Mullins was whether Congress can abolish the Federal Reserve System. His answer was:

The last provision of the Federal Reserve Act of 1913, Section 30, states: 'The right to amend, alter or appeal this Act is expressly reserved.' This language means that Congress can at any time move to abolish the Federal Reserve System or buy back this stock and make it a part of the Treasury Department, or to alter the System as it sees fit. It has never done so.

Congressman Louis McFadden of Pennsylvania, in Congressman McFadden on the Federal Reserve Corporation: Remarks in Congress, 1934, stated that "some people think that the Federal Reserve banks are U.S. Government institutions. They are not government institutions. They are private monopolies which prey upon the people of the United States for the benefit of themselves and their foreign customers."

In another citation, The Federal Reserve, a

Trillion Dollar Conspiracy, Gary Allen states, "The Federal Reserve controls our money, supply and interest rates, thereby manipulating the entire economy by creating inflation or deflation, recession or boom, and sending the stock market up or down at a whim." Allen goes on to say "much time and heat are consumed arguing over whether the Federal Reserve is private or publicly owned. The key point is not ownership of the System but control." Mr. Allen continues, commenting that "ownership of the Federal Reserve is not nearly so important as control. If you have the information in advance, there are vast opportunities for profit whichever direction the economy is going to move."

Earlier in this book, I spoke about unfair capitalism and the fact that there has been a polarization of the wealth in our country. Now I find information about the Federal Reserve System's control of the United States economy. Coincidence or synchronicity? This polarization has caused many poor people to "wish for more." Is one of the results of the wish for more mentality, the Los Angeles riots? What about the mugger who attacked my wife; was he wishing for more? Are the international bankers who control the Federal Reserve System to blame for these events?

Thus, I reasoned: is it really the white men and women against people of color? Or is it the haves against the havenots? Or is it a case of projection: international bankers see the poverty and misery of the people of color and reject them, when in actuality it is their own fear of poverty and misery that they hate! I am not a judge. You be the judge. Is it coincidence or synchronicity?

Sheldon Emry, previously referred to, says that "the credit for additional loans that is established by the Reserve banks, is what is known as our debt, and since the credit is illegal in the first place, and charging interest on loans is illegal, then our debt is illegal. The United States doesn't really have a national debt." He goes on to say:

The truth is the Federal Reserve's immense usury charges on their created credit (our debt), is the sole cause of inflation. All prices on all industry, trade and labor must be raised periodically to pay the ever-increasing usury charges. That is the only cause of higher prices and the money changers spend millions in propaganda to keep you from realizing that. The money creators (bankers) know that if we ever tried the constitutional issue of a debt free, interest free currency, even a limited issue, the benefits would be apparent immediately.

Emry also feels that "this creation of a phony debt has led many people to believe we have an obligation to pay off this debt, which, in reality, was only created at the whim of the Federal Reserve System." That system started in 1913 and has grown to a point where it has spiraled out of control. Last year the Federal

Reserve System, composed of private bankers, made $300 billion, states Emry. Now in my way of thinking, I am led to conclude that if the Federal Reserve function were returned to Congress and Congress ran the economic system as they were meant to, Congress could be the one making the $300 billion. It just seems like common sense.

I believe that the way the foregoing information came to me, without my specifically researching it, is a response to a particular incident: I had witnessed a car accident in which two Indian people had been drinking and one was killed. Later that summer at the Sun Dance, I had pulled seven buffalo skulls and had asked that the spirits give me an answer to why there is so much poverty and alcoholism on the reservations. I found that it is because of the economic system of this country, a system of unfair capitalism.

The Federal Reserve System is controlling the economy of the United States. They control the interest rate; they control Congress because most Congress-people are like willows who bend with the flow according to the "special interests." Congress has given the Federal Reserve the authority to run the economic system of our country. But they also have the right to change that function if they so desire. [3]

In the meantime, I have found that it's against God's law to charge interest on money lent. One cita-

3 *Ibid, pg.215.*

tion is from Exodus 22:25 and reads, "If thou lend money to any of my people that is poor by thee, thou shalt not be to him as an usurer, neither shalt thou lay upon him usury." And in Leviticus 25:36-37: "Take thou no usury of him, or increase...Thou shalt not give him thy money upon usury, nor lend him thy victuals for increase." God's law clearly states that interest is not to be charged on money lent. Yet, my discovery of what the Federal Reserve does is to, first, create money out of nothing, then turn around and charge interest on it. [4]

Gary Allen, in: Federal Reserve Between Dark and Conspiracy, lists the following as a way to eliminate the current U.S. economic problems. He says:

There is no painless solution to this problem, but to get out of this predicament with the least damage and dislocation we must do four things.

1. Taxes must be lowered and expenses cut by ending welfare to the lazy.
2. Deficit spending by the government must stop immediately.
3. The Federal Reserve note currency to date is illegal and unconstitutional. It must change. We must restore gold and silver backing behind our monetary system.
4. The Federal Reserve System, keystone of establishment socialism and the phony money in this country, must be abolished.

[4] *Ibid, pg.215.*

Lastly, he states, "The point is that the Federal Reserve cannot be reformed. You cannot reform something that is intrinsically wrong."

Because I believe that most politicians will always be swayed by special interests, I feel we would be wasting our time by contacting senators or representatives to demand a system change. [5]

In review, it seems that the international banking cartel has created an atmosphere whereby the whole world is "hooked" on credit. Most people in the United States buy everything on credit (money borrowed with interest). Our lifestyle is such that we do not want to sacrifice anything to correct the situation. We want to "have our cake and eat it, too." [6]

[5] *Ibid, pg.217.*
[6] *Ibid, pg.218.*

UNDERSTANDING THE "MEDIUM OF EXCHANGE"

In order to fully understand money, one needs to understand the "function" of money. The following is a satirical story on the fundaments of money. Long ago in a kingdom far away, the people would get things they needed by simply trading something they harvested for a product they did not have. Example: Potatoes for a duck. If the person who owned the duck did not want potatoes, then one had to trade something else or do work to get the duck. The goldsmith used gold to make things for trade because it is a soft metal he could make — cups, plates, jewelry — items he could trade for the food he needed. One day he had a great idea. Why not use gold as a medium of exchange? It was pretty, hard to get and he had lots of it. He talked to the king and proposed they be partners. The king liked the idea, so he declared gold as the "medium of exchange". Now the people were happy because they could work for this gold, or trade for the gold and anytime they wanted a duck they could just take gold to trade for it.

A small woman, who had a lot of gold, didn't feel safe because there were a lot of bandits in the woods. Since the goldsmith had an iron box where he kept his gold, she asked him to keep her gold for her. He said okay. Soon many people were putting their gold in his box. Now this woman had to go up a hill every day to trade her gold for bread. She became tired of carrying that heavy gold up the hill everyday. One day she had a great idea, why not just have the goldsmith write a note stating she had the gold in his box. The goldsmith wrote her this note; she took the note to the baker and traded it for the bread. This was a lot easier then hauling gold up the hill she thought. The goldsmith liked the idea too, because all the gold stayed in his box. The goldsmith told the king about the idea; the king liked the idea because he was partners with the goldsmith. So the king declared the note to be "money". Now these "notes" became the medium of exchange. The goldsmith soon became tired of writing notes for everyone so he started charging a fee to write notes. Now this seemed to be an easy way to get more gold he thought, so he had another idea. He told the king let's just start charging a fee anytime someone wants to borrow our money. The king jumped with joy and declared this fee to be called "interest".

What does this little story have to do with the Battle of the Little Big Horn? At the time of the Battle the Indians did not use money, theirs was a system of barter. Horses were a big part of that barter system. That's why there were approximately 22,000 ponies in their camp on June 25, 1876. Also just before the Battle, the army had paid their troops. Not having any place to spend this money, a majority of them had it with them when they went into the battle. After the battle as the

Indians were emptying the pockets of the dead, they had no use for the green "notes", so they just dumped it on the ground. There was approximately $25,000 blowing around the prairie that day. Later when the Indians surrendered, the army confiscated all their horses. Now I'm sure the battle of the Little Big Horn did not happen because the government wanted Indian horses. No, I think it was the gold they were after. The government needed the gold. Let me explain.

THE GOLDSMITH CHARGED A FEE

The scenario for the Battle of the Little Big Horn was set in motion 100 years previous to 1876 and it was in Europe! In 1773 Mayer Bauer of Frankfurt, Germany, invited 12 wealthy men into his goldsmith shop to convince them to pool their money so they could control the world. This was to be done by lending tremendous sums of money for a large interest rate. Bauer was only 30 years old at the time, later he changed his name to Rot-shild (Red Shield) which is the official crest of Frankfurt. Mayer Red Shield soon established a banking empire with banks in London, Paris, Amsterdam, Sweden, and Hamburg. These banks were eventually handed over to his five sons, Nathan, James, Leopold, Alfred, and Lionel. Two of his sons James of Paris and Nathan of London conceived a plan to make lots of money. Nathan had already made millions on the Battle of WaterLoo by tricking the financial people into dumping "notes" at low rates, then having his agents buy them. [7] Buy low sell high was the motto. Now the new plan was to create a civil war in America using the slavery issue. Nathan and James sent agents to America to "set the stage" for a civil war. By 1862 the stage was set, once the war began James would finance the South, charging a high interest rate and Nathan would do the

[7] *Mullins, The Secrets of the Federal Reserve, pg.55-57.*

same to the North. [8] But the plan failed when President Lincoln said no deal to the goldsmiths. Lincoln refused to pay the high rates of interest. Lincoln financed the war by printing Lincoln "Greenbacks". Money that had non-interest bearing notes. [9] The goldsmiths were furious. They created a financial panic which caused local financial agents to lobby Congress for a Bank Act which would not permit banks to create money as Lincoln had done. This resulted in the National Banking Act of 1864. [10] Because of Lincoln's greenbacks, there were rumors that a contract was put out on him. [11] The "goldsmiths" used agents to create the economic panic of 1873 by dumping "notes" and then buying them up a low rate. Also they began a move to ship all gold out of the country. [12] The government now needed gold to back their money. Where was the gold? In the Black Hills of South Dakota. But the Black Hills belonged to the Sioux. The agents now met with the government and together they planned to stampede the Black Hills with miners. Thus came Custer on the "Thieves Road" in 1874 to verify that there was gold in the Black Hills. [13] Next they needed a war against the Sioux to justify taking the Black Hills. Thus a call went out to the Powder River Indians

[8] Mullins, *The Curse of Canaan*, pg.150.
[9] Mullins, *The Secrets of the Federal Reserve*, pg.63-65.
[10] *Ibid*, pg.125.
[11] *Ibid*, pg.20
[12] *Ibid*, pg.125
[13] McMurtry, *Crazy Horse*, pg.77-79, pg.82.

to return to their reservations by January 31, 1876 or else be declared "hostile". [14] This the government did knowing the Indians could not travel in the dead of winter. So the Powder River Indians were declared hostiles and the war began. Is this the real cause for the Battle of the Little Big Horn? Is this coincidence or synchronicity? You be the judge. The result of the Battle of the Little Big Horn must have cause the "goldsmiths" (bankers) to jump for joy. Now they could lobby Congress to take the Black Hills away from the Sioux. This Congress did in 1876. It was called the Black Hills Agreement, but only Congress agreed on it. The amount of Sioux required to sign the agreement never did materialize. The "goldsmiths" had won.

[14] *Freedman, The Life and Death of Crazy Horse, pg.101-102.*

ALL THINGS ARE RELATED

As a student of Astrology, I realize that the influences that guide men are cyclic. These minute influences can best be explained by the Sioux concept of Mitakuye Oyasin, "Everything is Related". (For a more detailed explanation of Astrology, see pages 153-162 in Keeper of the Female Medicine Bundle 1998, by A.C. Ross)

I learned that everything that has a beginning, whether it be a concept, a person's life, or even the construction of an object, can be traced back to the movement of God's heavenly bodies. Therefore, I decided to ask my Astrologer Mary Jayn to do a star map on the Battle of the Little Big Horn based on the natal or birth time of the Battle. Gregory Michno in his excellent book on the Battle entitled Lakota Noon, said there is evidence that the Battle started at 1:00pm. [15] Since in the 1870's the United States did not have daylight savings time, the starting time for the Battle had to be adjusted 1 hour in order to get a current computer print out. The following is the computer print out with accompanying chart interpretation by Mary Jayn.

This is a chart of an event, which is interpreted differently than a natal chart.

---

[15] Michno, Lakota Noon, pg.XI of the Preface.

Little Big Horn Battle

Natal Chart
Jun 25 1876
2:00 PM   +7:09:51
Crow Agency
45N36 06 107W27 38
Geocentric
Tropical
Placidus
Mean Node

Compliments of:-
Mary Jayn
8527 West Colfax Avenue #208
Lakewood, CO 80215
(303) 232-8671

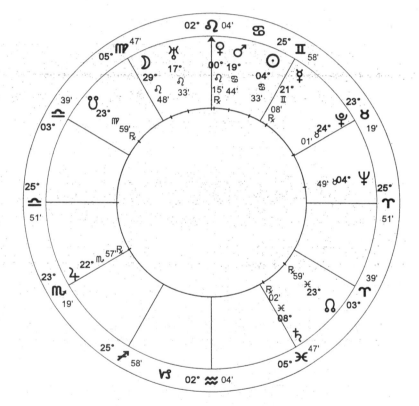

Because Libra is on the First House or the Ascendant of this chart, this is the aggressor - the U.S. Army. Because the ruler of Libra is Venus which is going backwards or is Retrograde [16] this indicates that the aggressor will not prevail nor win.

Because Venus is in the sign of Leo it indicates an aggressor who is proud, arrogant; because it is in 00 of Leo it means unpreparedness. [17]

Another meaning of a planet in an event chart which is Retrograde is that a similar event has happened before. [18]

The Indian Nation which was attacked is represented by the 7th house with Neptune in this part of the chart. Neptune is the planet of being taken advantage of, the underdog, those who have no power. [19]

Whenever an event is begun with the Moon void of course or at 29 degrees (usually) it indicates that the events will take a peculiar turn - very unpredictable and not anticipated. [20]

The attackers were inordinately intoxicated with pride and thought the outcome would be very different. Observe Jupiter sitting on the cusp of the second house

---

[16] *Retrograde implies the energy will be nullified.*

[17] *Custer was proud and arrogant.*

[18] *Custer attacked a large encampment under Black Kettle in 1878.*

[19] *American Indians were not made U.S. citizens until 1924; therefore they were powerless at the time of the Battle of the Little Big Horn.*

[20] *Custer attacked therefore he thought he could win, but unpredictable and not anticipated results occurred.*

in the death sign of Scorpio giving inordinate expectations of success. But Jupiter is Retrograde and in an event chart a planet which is Retrograde does not deliver. It falls short. [21]

Observe also that Pluto the death planet is in the 8th house (the death house) of this chart. The 8th house of this event chart indicates deaths of the aggressors. In addition this Pluto is sitting on the most malevolent star ALGOL at 24 Taurus - IN THE DEATH HOUSE. Most likely many deaths occurred through wounds to the throat and the chest. (Venus in Leo, Pluto in Taurus). This was a slaughter! [22] Jupiter in Scorpio opposed Pluto across the death axis.

The Nodes of the Moon are very karmic; they are destiny. [23] In this Battle chart, the South Node of the Moon meaning the past and connections with the past sits in the 11th part of the chart which means high hopes for the aggressor. This Node of the Moon is at 23 Scorpio 59 and is on the star Beta Leo which is "the persecutor."

Interestingly enough this placement of the South Node of the Moon from the Indian Nation's viewpoint lies on the house of creativity, and love. It appears that

---

[21] *Custer attacked therefore he thought he could win, but unpredictable and not anticipate results occurred.*
[22] *This explains Sitting Bull's vision and the premonitions of others.*
[23] *Karma is the law of "what you do to others, will be done to you". Custer had brutality killed Black Kettle and his people in 1868. Black Kettle was under a white flag of truce at the time of the attack.*

the Indian Nations through past accounts of the aggressor's activities realized that there was "no love lost" where the U.S. Army was concerned and regarded them as persecutors. [24] (the 11th house of the chart is the 5th from the 7th which represents the Indian Nations).

It is interesting to see some other heavenly bodies affecting the meaning of this chart. For example, the star Alpha Scorpius at 8 Sagittarius 00. The meaning of this star is "obsession leads to downfall." [25] The placement of this star is in the immediate future of the aggressor (the second house). In addition, in astrology there is a way to calculate degrees of the zodiac associated with certain meanings. It is interesting to note that the degree of the zodiac indicating the Part of Catastrophe is - also exactly at 8 Sagittarius 00.

To sum up these two meanings, the aggressor through miscalculation, obsession with being right and disregarding the rights of others walked into catastrophe. [26]

The Part of Spirit in this chart is 00 Scorpio 00. Within minutes, here the Moon of this chart will trigger this degree. Mary Jayn asked sarcastically did the Spirits assist?

---

[24] *Manifest Destiny was a term created by the white man to justify their treatment of the American Indian.*
[25] *They were obsessed with getting the gold in the Black Hills; this led to Custer's defeat.*
[26] *Unchecked manifest destiny led to Custer's undoing.*

My Astrologer told me that before she did this star map or natal chart on the Battle of the Little Big Horn, she had not heard of the Battle. She had heard of Custer but did not know he was involved in the Battle, of course she knew nothing of the Indians involved in the Battle. When I explained what happened at the Battle, she exclaimed this is the exact information she got from the Battle chart! In answering her question did the spirits assist? My answer is an unequivocal, Yes they did. Let us look at signs that have led me to this decision.

1. Sitting Bull, Hunkpapa Medicine Man; had a Sun Dance vision on June 5, 1876, he saw soldiers falling into camp, a great omen of victory.

2. Cheyenne Holy man, Box Elder, dreamed two days before the Battle that soldiers were coming.

3. After an officer's meeting with Custer the eve of June 22, 1876 Lieutenant Wallace told Lieutenant Ed Godfrey he felt Custer would not live long.

4. On June 24, 1876, the 7th Cavalry came across the Hunkpapa Sun Dance ground of June 5th, when Custer's HDQ flag was thrust into the ground. All of a sudden it fell over backwards all by itself. So the guidon thrust the flag into the ground a second time, only to have it mysteriously fall backwards again.

5. On June 24th as the Arikara scouts were examining the sweat lodge remains they discovered signs that Custer was about to lose a battle.

6. On the morning of the Battle, June 25, 1876, Custer's favorite scout, an Arikara named Bloody Knife predicted he would not see the sun set that day.
7. On the morning of the Battle, Oglala Holy man Black Elk had a premonition that a great Battle was about to happen. [27]

Now if you told these premonitions to an Indian of that period they would have known instantly to beware. I am sure that even today those Indians who are raised closest to their culture would have the same reaction. Most whiteman are not taught to appreciate their instincts.

Research done on brain hemispericy states that each side of the brain is dominant in different modes of thought: The left is logical, linear, verbal, sequential, and masculine thought. The right is instinctive, wholistic, non-verbal, spatial and feminine thought.

My research into brain hemispericy indicates that modern society and especially our school systems place stress on the modes of thought connected with the left side of the brain more than the right side. Consequently modern man is taught to place an emphasis on books and libraries as the source of all knowledge. By contrast, in traditional Sioux culture, any time a person wanted knowledge or information, he attend-

[27] *Michno, Lakota Noon, pg.33*

ed a ceremony and requested the information from the spirit world via an Iyeska (Holy man). [28]

So based on the study of astrology and my own actual experience in this type of phenomenon I would have to say yes to my Astrologers question on spiritual involvement in the Battle of the Little Big Horn. The position of the heavenly bodies on that day did determine the outcome. Custer died for the sins of the "goldsmiths". Indeed the influences that guide men are cyclic. [29]

[28] *Ross, Mitakuye Oyasin "We are all Related", pg.11-25.*
[29] *The heavenly bodies are in constant movement, advancing 30 degrees every 2,300 years.*

ONE THOUSAND YEARS OF PEACE

ONE THOUSAND YEARS OF PEACE

In Oglala Religion by William K. Powers, Dakota/Lakota language structures identified that separate lexical categories are not employed to differentiate between time and space. Time and space are inseparable. All temporal statements in the Dakota/Lakota languages are simultaneously spatial. Example: A simple sentence in Lakota is, "Letan Pine Ridge towhan hwo." The Literal English interpretation is "When is Pine Ridge from here?" But in the English language, the same sentence is usually stated, "How far is it to Pine Ridge?" indicating left-brain dominance. Thus, in the Lakota language, the spatial or right brain orientation is dominant.

Marilyn Ferguson said in the Aquarian Conspiracy that European languages trap us in a model of understanding that is piecemeal. They pay no attention to relationships by their subject/predicate structure, thus molding our thought patterns by making us think in terms of simple cause and effect. She further stated that, "...for this reason it is hard for us to talk about or even think about quantum physics, the fourth dimension, or any other notion without clear-cut beginning and ending, up and down, then and now."

Modern science has discovered that there is something in the cosmos that is not in accord with the concepts that modern man has formed. Charlton

Laird's book Language in America recorded that linguist Benjamin Whorf suggested that the Hopi language, if it will not help scientists find a new language they need, may at least help them see what is wrong with the old one. My interpretation of this is that Native American languages allow more right-brain expression, whereas European languages encourage almost solely left-brain expression.

A Hopi prophecy told about two brothers - one white and a one red. The white brother went to the other side of the planet and will return one day. When he comes back, the two brothers will sit down together and learn each other's language. After that, their two lifeways will entwine and become one.

When I heard this prophecy, what first occurred to me was the information about the left and right hemispheres of the brain. To me, the white brother would be left-brain dominant, and the red brother would be right-brain dominant because of their differing language structures. After we learn each other's ways, we will become whole-brain thinkers. [1]

Hopi spiritual leader Dan Katchongva stated that if the races become separated from each other and no longer know their original teachings, the Creator would cause three world-shaking events to remind them that "we are all related." The story connected to

[1] Ross, Mitakuye Oyasin, "We are all Related", pg.56-57.

Hopi Prophecy Rock Petroglyph

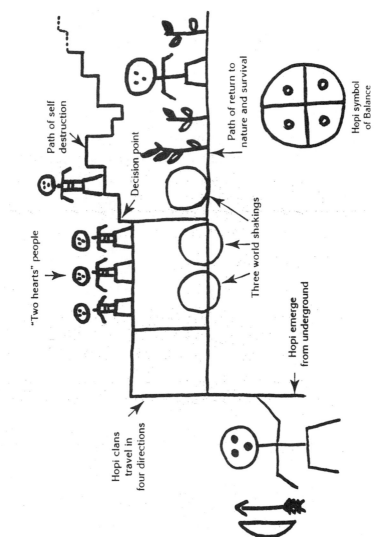

the Hopi prophecy rock tells of a time when the Hopi emerged from the underground. The leading clans went in the four directions, then turned right, thus forming a Swastika symbol. The leading clans were: Fire, Spider, Eagle, Kachina, Bear, Badger, Flute, Snake.

The second group of clans which came out of the underground also went out in the four directions, then turned left, thus forming a Swastika in the opposite direction. These clans were named: Butterfly, Bluebird, Crow, Crane, Corn, Pumpkin, Sun, Lizard.

As the Hopi spread knowledge and information around the world, people would gradually become "two hearts," people who think with their head rather than their hearts.

Is it coincidence or synchronicity that the people of Earth today are left brain dominant? Left-brain dominant is to use rational thinking only versus the right-brain function of intuitive thinking. The Hopi prophecy rock goes on to show how man will reach a point where he can make a decision to either continue on the road of thinking with his head only or return to the road of thinking with his heart. If we continue thinking with our head only (rational), we will eventually destroy ourselves. If we take the road of thinking with our heart (intuition) we will eventually return to respect for nature and our survival. On the prophecy rock are also three circles, which represent the three world-shaking events (purifications) which are to remind us of our relativeness. Each of the shakings would be accompanied by a symbol. The symbol for the first shaking would be a "bug on a black ribbon being tossed into the sky." This was interpreted as an airplane. The time when airplanes were first used in war was World War I. So this was the first world shaking. The symbol for the second shaking would be when man used the Hopi migration symbol (Swastika) for war. This was in World War II. So this was the second world shaking. The symbol for the third world shaking would be the color red (a red covering of cloak). Will there be a World War III? The Hopi prophecy rock predicts the third shaking to be a time of total destruction or total rebirth. It is interesting to note that Nostradamus predicted World War III to start January 1991 and to last for ten years. The Hopi say that signs of the third shaking would be when:

1. Trees will die (unknown disease kills palm trees in Florida).
2. Man will build a house in the sky (sky lab?).
3. Cold places become hot, and hot places become cold (global warming?)
4. Land will sink, and land will rise (volcanoes in Iceland cause new land?).
5. There is an appearance of the Blue Star Kachina (Hale-Bopp?).

The Hopi say man needs to return to the original teachings if we want to survive the third world shaking. [2]

Chief Seattle of the Suquamish, when asked by the government to sell the tribe's land stated the following. These are excerpts from his speech, which was titled, "How can one sell the air?"

We will consider your offer to buy our land.

Do not send men asking us to decide more quickly. We will decide in our time.

Should we accept, I here and now make this condition: we will never be denied the right to walk softly over the grave of our fathers, mothers, and friends, nor may the white man desecrate these graves.

The graves must always be open to the sunlight and the falling rain.

Then the water will fall gently upon the green sprouts and sleep slowly down to moisten the parched lips of our ancestors and quench their thirst.

Every part of this earth is sacred to my people.

Every hillside, every valley, every clearing and wood, is holy in the memory and experience of my people.

Even those unspeaking stones along the shore are loud with the events and memories in the life of my people.

[2] *Ibid, pg.226-228.*

The ground beneath your feet responds more lovingly to our steps than yours, because it is the ashes of our grandfathers.

Our bare feet know the kindred touch.

The earth is rich with the lives of our kin.

Men come and go, like the waves of the sea.

A tear, a prayer to the Great Spirit, a dirge (lament), and they are gone from our longing eyes forever.

Even the white man, whose God walked and talked with him as friend to friend, cannot be exempt from the common destiny.

We may be brothers after all. We shall see. [3]

Black Elk said the 7th holy rite of the Oglala was the "throwing of the ball ceremony." This game represented man's life. He said the playing field stood for the universe; the center of the playing field represented Wakan Tanka or God. The ball also represented Wakan Tanka. The buffalo had no hands and couldn't catch the ball, a representation of ignorance or walking the Black Road.

In The Sacred Pipe Joseph Epes Brown recorded Black Elk's words:

"I, Black Elk, should now explain to you several things that you may not understand about his holy rite. First, it is a little girl, and not an older person, who stands at the center and who throws the ball. This is as

[3] *Ibid, pg.228-231.*

it should be, for just as Wakan Tanka is eternally youthful and pure, so is this little one who has just come from Wakan Tanka, pure and without any darkness. Just as the ball is thrown from the center to the four quarters, so Wakan Tanka is at every direction and is everywhere in the world; and as the ball descends upon the people, so does His power, which is only received by a very few people, especially in these last days.

"You have seen that the four-legged buffalo people were not able to play this game with the ball, and so they gave it to the two legged. This is very true because, as I have said before, of all the created things or beings of the universe, it is the two-legged men alone who, if they purify and humiliate themselves, may become one with - or may know - Wakan Tanka.

"At his sad time today among our people we are scrambling for the ball, and some are not even trying to catch it, which makes me cry when I think of it. But soon I know it will be caught, for the end is rapidly approaching, and then it will be returned to the center, and our people will be with it. It is my prayer that this be so, and it is in order to aid in this 'recovery of the ball', that I have wished to make this book." [4]

Just before Black Elk's death in the early 1950s, he prophesied that soon someone would catch the ball (become one with Wakan Tanka). In the process of catching it, that person would return it to the center of

[4] *Ibid, pg.104.*

the playing field (center of the universe). This prophecy reminded me of how Dawson No Horse received his power.

Dawson told me that in 1974, while he was still an Episcopal priest, he was drawn to attend the Sun Dance. While observing it, he saw a person standing in the center by the tree. He asked someone standing next to him, "Who is that standing out there?" The man replied, "I don't see anybody."

Wanting an explanation for this vision, Dawson went to Frank Fools Crow, an Oglala holy man. Frank immediately recognized what was happening and told Dawson to fast on the hill for four days and four nights. Dawson said that the first three days, nothing happened-he was only aware of his hunger, his thirst, and insects eating at him. On the fourth day, a thunderstorm appeared and a bolt of lightning came out of the storm and struck right beside him. The man he had seen in his vision at the Sun Dance stood where the lightning had struck. This man's name was Canupa Gluha Mani (Walks with the Pipe).

After Dawson came down from the hill, Fools Crow started teaching him yuwipi songs and how to conduct the ceremony because he knew that Dawson was suppose to become a yuwipi man (a holy man). Canupa Gluha Mani was Dawson's main spirit helper in the yuwipi ceremony.

For seven years Dawson held ceremonies in which hundreds of people were healed. He carried the ball or walked with God for seven years. Then he told his family, "They're calling me on the other side. It's time for me to go." His family said, "Don't talk like that."

"I know that a lot of these things I have done you have a hard time believing," he replied, "but I tell you now that it's time for me to go." And he planned his own funeral. He said all people were welcome to attend, no matter what religion, no matter what race. On January 28, 1982, the body of Dawson Has No Horse died. I believe his spirit returned to the center of the universe. [5]

Black Elk's explanation of the seventh rite and the information coming from the collective unconscious of Edgar Cayce concerning reincarnation, were almost the same. Cayce said that a person is reincarnated again and again until he becomes whole. Each incarnation is an opportunity for the individual to grow and expand. Cayce stated that when one has fulfilled his karmic debts (sins committed in this life and previous lives), then that individual becomes one with God and his will conforms with the will of the Creator, his earthly cycles are finished, and his soul may return to the center of the universe. Is this what happened to Dawson? Did he

[5] *Ibid, pg.105.*

become one with God? Is Dawson the person who fulfilled Black Elk's prophecy? [6]

In Dakota spirituality, the earth was considered feminine and the people called her Mother Earth. The Dakota hero archetype was also considered feminine and is known as the White Buffalo Calf Maiden. Almost all tribes have a female as their Hero Archetype. The Hopi have Corn Mother, the Navajo have Changing Women, the Taos have Deer Mother, and the Iroquois have the Three Sisters. Cherokee have Corn Women and Apache have White Painted Mother. In The Portable Jung by Joseph Campbell, he states that in the early Christian church, the Trinity was symbolized by a dove named Sophia, which was a feminine entity!

How did modern man become so out of balance in the way he views the world? Was it when he invented a written language? Or was it when he invented time references (calendar/clock)? Or was it when he invented money (which has lead to economic theories)? All of these inventions utilize left brain modes of thought. Consequently, we live in a left brain dominant world (masculine oriented).

According to Rayna Green, author of Women in American Indian Society, information about American Indian women was first documented by the European white male chauvinist, who possessed religious bigotry.

---

[6] *Ibid, pg.106.*

Therefore, a clear picture of early American Indian women did not emerge. The truth is that upon the arrival of the European, native women enjoyed suffrage, sexual liberation, social status of matriarchy, and economic independence (since they did the work, they owned the produce/products). At the completion of Dakota ceremonies, we say Mitakuye Oyasin, which in its spiritual context means everything is related. Traditionally, all planting societies were matriarchal and all hunting societies were patriarchal. After the Lakota acquired the horse, their culture slowly changed from that of a planting society to that of the hunter. But the respect for the feminine has remained among our people. According to the psychic prophet Edgar Cayce, "Entropy of the masculine and feminine energy would begin in 1933. At that time, souls of an androgynous nature would enter the new born bodies here on earth." This may be the reason for male bodies acting more feminine and female bodies acting masculine nowadays. This is good because it provides a balance of the Anima (female) within the male, and the Animus (male) within the female. Edgar Cayce states that the influx of the androgynous souls would continue for 100 years. These androgynous bodies will be the next root race to enter earth's plane, and they will create the thousand years of peace of which the Bible speaks. [7]

[7] *Ross, Keeper of the Female Medicine Bundle, pg.229-231.*

In the old days, a person would go on a vision quest to find out what he was good at or what his purpose in life might be. Today, we use astrology. Astrology is a picture of the heavens the moment you are born. From this picture or Star Map, a skilled astrologer can determine a person's inclinations for his life. As we move into the next century, I feel that astrology is a valuable tool that could be used in education. In the old days, astrology was considered a joke and teaching was by reward and punishment.

Nowadays, there is a change happening. This shift, which is called "Entropy" in psychological terms, will continue until completed. It is a natural evolutionary cycle. So it is best that we recognize this, accept it, and assist it until balance has been achieved. [8]

Ho Hecetu Yelo
"That's the way it is"

[8] *Ibid, pg.237-238.*

EPILOGUE

We have entered into a new millennium and according to those who study the heavens, we are now being influenced by the energy of peace, unity, and brotherhood.

The financial abuses mentioned in this book happened over one hundred years ago. Since then new laws against monopoly and insider trading have been installed. I'm sure Ivan Boesky, Mike Milken, and Bill Gates can all assert to that fact. Even the issue of an "interest rate" is changing. Last week I got a letter from a credit card company that stated it would give me a 1.9% interest rate on all balance transfers, a change from the previous 12.9% rate. Also mankind is experiencing a rise in the feminine energy. It has been predicted that there will be less fighting and killings. A few days ago, I saw a program on television where the U.S. Marines went on a rescue mission in Somalia using rubber bullets! When I was growing up in South Dakota there was a tremendous amount of animosity between the white man and the Indian. This too has changed, a century ago Crazy Horse was treated as a villain, today he is a hero, as the races educated themselves through books and culture courses. Respect for one another can only get better and we owe all the thanks to the influences from heaven.

Mitakuye Oyasin
"We are all related"

APPENDIX A

ART WORK

    Drawn by Martin Red Bear, Oglala/Sichangu,
Professor, Oglala Sioux College, Kyle. S.D.

CHARTS

    Drawn by A.C. Ross, computer enchanced by
Jonathan Canady, Sir Speedy, Lakewood, CO.

MAPS

    Drawn by A.C. Ross, computer enhanced by
Jonathan Canady, Sir Speedy, Lakewood CO.,

    Source: Bozeman Trail map
               Freedman, Russell <u>The Life and Death of Crazy Horse</u>, p.61
               Ft. Laramie Treaty- 1863 map
               Ortiz, Roxann Dunbar, <u>The Great Sioux Nation</u>, p.92

APPENDIX B

THE RECTIFICATION AND ANALYSIS OF THE HOROSCOPE OF CRAZY HORSE
by Mary R. Jayn

THE RECTIFICATION PROCESS

The Rectification of a birth chart is an exercise for an astrological detective. One must visit the past and from the paths of the planets, select the year, month, day, and time of birth which reflect the potentials of the individual in question.

History records Crazy Horses' involvement in significant battles, meetings in Great Councils, his arrest and death. Many of these events record the month, day, and year. From these clues and from reports of his character and other pieces of information, a sense of character evolves and takes shape.

In this particular case, this horoscope must show an individual who would be martyred as a result of circumstance fulfilling his goal to preserve things as they are. It must show one who quietly communed with nature, who was spiritual, taciturn — yet a man of action. And, it must reflect a man who was his own person — the deviant one.

With these parameters a test chart emerges against which the chart is tested for accuracy. For example, using Solar Arc measurements [1] one can assess how the horoscope responds to certain events. Then, the transits of the planets are applied to the test chart for verification. From this assessment the month and day can be determined.

Using these main parameters and the information from Dr. A. Ross Ehanamani's spirit guides, I have rectified Crazy Horses' birth to be: May 5, 1840; 8:28:56 am; 34N54; 102W36.

HOROSCOPE ANALYSIS

With Sun in Taurus and Moon in Cancer this is a person whose main drive was to preserve the status-quo to gain security for himself and his people. This Sun Moon placement gives a stubborn streak within the character; one who won't yield easily.

With Cancer rising and with the Moon in Cancer, he felt responsible for actually feeding his own — which he did. Cancer rising gives an attachment to one's own family which was his people.

Pattern placement of the planets in Crazy Horse's chart are top heavy — the emphasis is above the horizon. This indicates that despite his choice of the quiet life, communing with nature in his own way,

[1] *A technique involving yearly movement of the natal Sun as the basis, or increment of movement. This increment is applied yearly to every planet according to the time frame in question.*

circumstances would deem otherwise. This planetary placement indicates victimization. Who would say otherwise?

This is a feeling individual. Note the Moon in its own sign on the Ascendant AND peregrine [2]. The feeling level, the attachment to family, and the need to feel secure within these constructs is emphasized.

One aspect (165°) from the Moon to Saturn in the 6th house indicates an obsessive need to take care of his family and he considered this his work. (Saturn is in the 6th of work and in the principled sign of Sagittarius).

Status to Crazy Horse was irrelevant. He listened to the voice within. His Sun, Mars conjunction in Taurus is square to Neptune in the 8th. This is ego relinquishment. Furthermore, the sign Pisces lies on the Midheaven of this chart — this is martyrdom.

[2] *No sextile, square, opposition, conjunction, or trine to any other planets.*

To pursue his belief system more thoroughly, note that Uranus is in the 9th but very close to the Midheaven — its most powerful position. Uranus is in mutual reception with Neptune in the 8th. In other words, Uranus is in Pisces which is Neptune's sign. Neptune is in Aquarius which is Uranus' sign. A mutual reception emphasizes the importance of the planets. In this case, Spirit (Neptune) reinforced belief (Uranus) and translated it into a defiant person.

This person emerges because Uranus is closely square Saturn — one who is defiant, one who resists authority. Historically, those born with Uranus square Saturn are those individuals who are in the teetering brink of societal change. These are the ones who pay the price of changing society.

Although Taurus can represent an individual who could be taciturn, in this chart Pluto is conjunct Mercury which accounts for Crazy Horses' being a "man of few words." With Venus, Pluto, and Mercury all conjunct in Aries, Crazy Horse would say, "What you do, speaks louder that what you say."

Crazy Horses' death and the circumstances which surround it speaks eloquently from this chart. The fourth house — the end of things and of life — is ruled by Virgo in this chart. Virgo is ruled by Mercury which also rules the 12th house of betrayal and secret enemies.

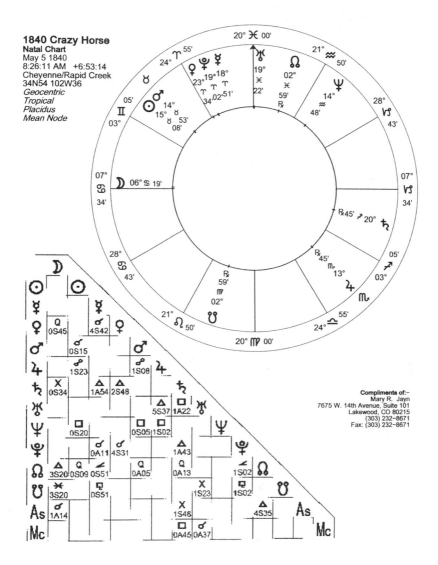

1840 Crazy Horse
Natal Chart
May 5 1840
8:26:11 AM   +6:53:14
Cheyenne/Rapid Creek
34N54 102W36
Geocentric
Tropical
Placidus
Mean Node

Compliments of:—
Mary R. Jayn
7675 W. 14th Avenue, Suite 101
Lakewood, CO 80215
(303) 232-8671
Fax: (303) 232-8671

105

APPENDIX C

A tentative genealogy of Crazy Horse

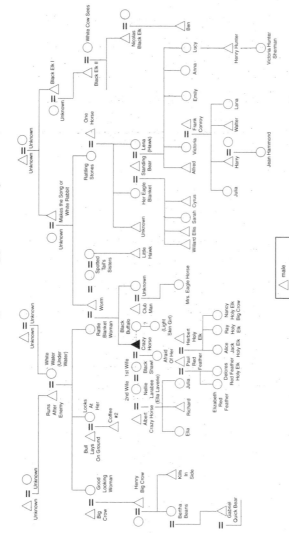

This chart was provided by Ben "Butch" Sherman.
His lineage is from Rattling Stones woman.
She was Crazy Horse's Paternal Aunt (Worm's Sister).

106

APPENDIX D

LENGTH OF THE BATTLE

	INDIANS	SOLDIERS
RENO ATTACKS	9:30 (approximate)	1:00 pm
SOLDIERS IN THE NORTH	10:30 (approximate)	2:00 pm
SOLDIERS ARE SURROUNDED	11:30 (approximate)	3:20 pm
LAST STAND	12:00 (approximate)	4:20 pm

Note: The Mniconju White Bull stated the Battle Started at mid-morning (9:00 or 10:00) and lasted until noon [1]
Official inquiry by the Army stated the Battle started at 1:00 pm, far west time, [2] and lasted three hours.[3]

[1] Hardorff, Richard G., _Lakota Recollections of the Custer fight_, p.40
[2] Ibid, p.40
[3] Michno, _Gregory F. Lakota noon_, p. xi

BIBLIOGRAPHY

Clark, Robert A. The Killing of Chief Crazy Horse.
Lincoln/London: University of Nebraska Press, 1976.

Freedman, Russell. The Life and Death of Crazy Horse.
New York: Holiday House, 1996.

Hardorff, Richard G. Lakota Recollections of the Custer Fight.
Lincoln/London: University of Nebraska Press, 1997.

Henckel, Mark. The Battle of the Little Big Horn.
Billings/Helena, Montana, Falcon Press, 1992.

Howard, H.P. Crazy Horse - Tashunka Witko.
Pamphlet, copyright 1975.

Kadlecek, Edward and Mabell. To Kill an Eagle.
Boulder: Johnson Books, 1981.

McMurtry, Larry. Crazy Horse.
New York: Viking Penquin, 1999.

Michno, Gregory F. Lakota Noon. The Indian Narrative of
Custer's Defeat.
Missoula, Montana: Mountain Press, 1997.

Mullins, Eustace. The Secrets of the Federal Reserve.
Staunton, Virgina: Banker's Research Institute, 1993.

Mullins, Eustace. The Curse of Canaan.
Staunton, Virginia: Revelation Books, 1987.

Ross, Allen. Mitakuye Oyasin "We are all related".
Denver, Colorado: Wicòni Wastè, 1999, 14th Printing.

Ross, Allen. Ehanamani "Walks Among".
Denver, Colorado: Wicòni Wastè, 1997, 4th Printing.

Ross, Allen. Keeper of the Female Medicine Bundle.
Denver, Colorado: Wicòni Wastè, 1999, 3rd Printing.

Sandoz, Mari. Crazy Horse - Strange Man of the Oglala.
Lincoln/London: University of Nebraska Press, 1992.

Van Nuys, Maxell. Inkpaduta - The Scarlet Point.
Denver, Colorado: Maxell Van Nuys, 1998.

Wilson, D.Ray. Wyoming Historical Guide.
Carpentersville, Illinois: Crossroads Communication, 1990, 2nd Edition.

VIDEO

Archaeology, History and Custer's Last Battle with Richard A. Fox Ph.D.   Hardin, Montana: El Conejo Productions, 1995.

MITAKUYE OYASIN

"we are all related"

The history and culture of America before Columbus, based on American Indian oral history. Twenty-six years of research have gone into this book. It is the doctorate dissertation of Lakota Sioux author, Ehanamani "walks among."

The book **MITAKUYE OYASIN** by Ehanamani A. C. Ross compares the legends and cultures of the American Indian with the world's major philosophies and religions.

Topics include:

- Esoteric teachings of the American Indian
- Brain hemisphercy and cultural attitudes
- Spiritual healing
- Black Elk's prophecy
- Strategies for global harmony
- American Indian philosophy
- Origins of the American Indian

MITAKUYE OYASIN
"We are all related"
REVISED EDITION

Dr. A.C. Ross
(Ehanamani)

OVER 60,000 COPIES SOLD

Winner of the 1992 "top 50" Recognition Award at the Frankfurt International Bookfair, **MITAKUYE OYASIN** is being used in over 50 universities and 300 high schools in the areas of: psychology, comparative religions, native American studies, philosophy, counseling and guidance.

In its twelfth printing, the book is a best seller in Europe with translations in French, Russian, German, Japanese and Italian.

A teacher's guide is also available.

ISBN 0-9621977-0X $12.00

The Dakota/Lakota author of *Mitakuye Oyasin* shares a

SUN DANCE EXPERIENCE

This experience led him to discover how American Indian poverty

IS PERPETUATED BY THE FEDERAL RESERVE SYSTEM!

Follow the Ehanamani family from 1863 when it was forced onto the reservation and learn about reservation life from 1940 to the present.

You'll learn:

- The *real reason* behind the slogan "Indian Giver."
- About the Chief Big Foot Ride Prophecy.
- About the Serpent Vision.
- What the term *walk-in* means.
- Where the Bible condemns the charging of interest on monetary loans.
- How encounters of the fourth kind are guiding us into the Future.

ISBN 0-9621977-2-6 $12.00

Ehanamani
"Walks Among"

The Winter Count
of a Santee Dakota Educator,
Historian, and Spiritual Guide

Chronology of Highlights in the
Life of Ehanamani

- Born at Pipestone
- Return from Death
- Serpent Vision
- U.S. Paratrooper
- Sun Dance Vision
- Grass Dance Champ
- Big Foot Ride Prophecy

Traditionally, a Winter Count was the pictorial history of a tribe or individual. Each picture represented the most important event of the year.

AMERICAN INDIAN PROPHECIES I

(Ojibwa, Hopi, Paiute, Sioux, Maya, Navajo, and Aztec)

Compared with predictions by:

NOSTRADAMUS
EDGAR CAYCE
RUTH MONTGOMERY
GORDON-MICHAEL SCALLION

Produced by Wicóni Wasté
Narrated by Dr. A.C. Ross
Author of <u>Mitakuye Oyasin</u>
"We are all related"

DISCOVER:

Δ How to prepare for the coming earth changes
Δ How the Black Hills can be returned
Δ When spiritual unity will occur
Δ What to invest money in for the future
Δ What is causing the increase in earthquakes, volcanic
   eruptions, and unknown diseases

<u>MAIL ORDER</u>

HOME VIDEO

VHS - $19.95 + $3.95(S&H) = $23.90
PAL (European) - $29.95 + $8.95(S&H) = $38.90
(We accept Visa/MC)

SEND TO: **Wicóni Wasté " Beautiful Life"**
              P.O. Box 480005
              Denver, CO 80248
              303-238-3420

AMERICAN INDIAN PROPHECIES I

Sun Dance Vision

Produced by:
Wicóni Wasté
Running Time 1 hr.

AMERICAN INDIAN PROPHECIES II

An Interview With "Ehanamani"
a.k.a.
Dr. A.C. Ross

Due to popular demand, Dr. Ross discusses the prophecies presented in the video, American Indian Prophecies I

Interviewer: John Belindo

Issues to be Discussed:

Δ Return of the White Buffalo
Δ The Mayan calendar's connection to the "Quickening."
Δ Biblical prophecy comparisons
Δ When will spiritual unity occur
Δ Will Tribal Governments survive
Δ Black Elk's Vision of the Flowering Tree
Δ Who is guiding us into the next century

HOME VIDEO

VHS - $19.95 + $3.95(S&H) = $23.90
PAL (European) - $29.95 + $8.95(S&H) = $38.90

(We accept Visa/MC)

SEND TO: Wicóni Wasté " Beautiful Life "
P.O. Box 480005
Denver, CO 80248
303-238-3420

MAIL ORDER

AMERICAN INDIAN PROPHECIES II

The White Buffalo

Pleiades (HEAD)

Betelgeuse (RIB)

Orion's Belt (BACKBONE)

Sirius (TAIL)

Rigel (RIB)

Produced by:
Wicóni Wasté
Running Time 1 hr.

AMERICAN INDIAN PROPHECIES III

An Interview With "Ehanamani"
a.k.a.
Dr. A.C. Ross

Due to popular demand, Dr. Ross discusses
additional prophecies

Interviewer: Jeff D. Alley

MAIL ORDER

Issues to be Discussed:

Δ Black Elk's Sacred Hoop of Nations Vision
Δ Will the Sweat Lodge Ceremony Survive?
Δ Dawson No Horse Vision of the Future
Δ Prophecy of the androgynous beings
Δ What is meant by "medium of exchange"
Δ A dream about the American Indian Prophecy videos
Δ Wounded Knee memorial ride prophecy

HOME VIDEO

VHS - $19.95 + $3.95 (S&H) = $23.90
PAL (European) - $29.95 + $8.95 (S&H) = $38.90
(We accept Visa/MC)

SEND TO: **Wicóni Wasté "Beautiful Life"**
P.O. Box 480005
Denver, CO 80248
303-238-3420

AMERICAN INDIAN PROPHECIES III
Wicóni Wasté – copyright 1996

AMERICAN INDIAN PROPHECIES III

*Wounded Knee Memorial Ride
Prophecy*

Produced by:
Wicóni Wasté
Running Time 55 min.

HALE – BOPP
COMET OR STAR?

A Presentation by Ehanamani

a.k.a.

Dr. A.C. Ross

A Comparison of information concerning the HALE – BOPP comet.

Topics Presented:

Δ Learn the correlation between the Blue Star and the comet Hale – Bopp.

Δ What do the Hopi / Lakota have in common with the Blue Star.

Δ Discover the connection between the Bible and Hale – Bopp

Δ Is Hale – Bopp a harbinger for destruction or peace?

Δ Why has NASA discontinued publishing information concerning Hale – Bopp?

Δ Is there a correlation between Hale – Bopp and the 12th planet?

Δ Learn how Hale – Bopp is ushering in the second coming.

HOME VIDEO

VHS - $19.95 + $3.95(S&H) = $23.90

PAL (European) - $29.95 + $8.95(S&H) = $38.90

(We accept Visa/MC)

MAIL ORDER

SEND TO: **Wicóni Wasté "Beautiful Life"**
P.O. Box 480005
Denver, CO 80248
303-238-3420

ISBN 0-9621977-6-9

9 780962 197765

AMERICAN INDIAN PROPHECIES IV

HALE – BOPP
PROPHECY STAR?

Produced by:
Wicóni Wasté
Running Time 1 hour

VIDEO
MAIL ORDER FORM

American Indian Prophecy Videos I, II, III and IV

<table>
<tr><td colspan="4" align="center">ORDER FORM</td></tr>
<tr><td colspan="4">Name _____</td></tr>
<tr><td colspan="4">Address _____</td></tr>
<tr><td colspan="4">City _____ State _____ Zip _____</td></tr>
<tr><td>Qty</td><td>Title</td><td>Price/Video</td><td>Total</td></tr>
<tr><td></td><td>VIDEO</td><td>$19.95 EA</td><td></td></tr>
<tr><td></td><td>SET (4 VIDEOS)</td><td>$59.95 EA</td><td></td></tr>
<tr><td></td><td></td><td></td><td></td></tr>
<tr><td colspan="4" align="center">POSTAGE (BOOK RATE)</td></tr>
<tr><td></td><td>VIDEO</td><td>$ 3.95 EA</td><td></td></tr>
<tr><td></td><td>1 SET (4 VIDEOS)</td><td>$ 5.95</td><td></td></tr>
<tr><td></td><td>Handling ($1.50 per order)</td><td></td><td>$ 1.50</td></tr>
<tr><td colspan="4" align="center">TOTAL</td></tr>
</table>

Air Mail: For orders from outside the USA, add $5.00 per video. For orders from outside North America, add $8.00 per video.

Make checks, money orders and purchase orders payable to:

Wicóni Wasté – "Beautiful Life"
PO BOX 480005
DENVER, CO 80248
303-238-3420

CREDIT CARD ORDERS WELCOMED (VISA/MC)

BOOKS

ORDER FORM

Name _____

Address _____

City _____ State _____ Zip _____

Qty	Title	Price	Total
	EHANAMANI	$12.00 EA	
	MITAKUYE OYASIN	$12.00 EA	
	KEEPER - FEMALE BUNDLE	$14.95	
	CRAZY HORSE	$10.95	
	SUBTOTAL		
		Postage (see below)	
	Handling ($1.50 per order)		$1.50
	TOTAL		

Postage (Priority)
1-4 copies $3.20
5 or more copies   .80 per book

Air Mail: For orders outside the U.S., add $5.00 per book. For
other international orders, add $8.00 per book.

Make checks, money orders and
purchase orders payable to:
    Wicóni Wasté
    P.O. BOX 480005
    DENVER, CO 80248

For wholesale orders, contact:
    New Leaf Distributing
    401 Thornton Road
    Lithia Springs, GA 30122

CREDIT CARD ORDERS WELCOMED

ABOUT THE AUTHOR

   Ehanamani (Walks Among) aka A.C. Ross has worked for 27 years in the field of education as a teacher, principal, superintendent, college professor and college department chairman. He left formal education 7 years ago to promote his book entitled _Mitakuye Oyasin_ _"We Are All Related"_. It won the top book award at Europe's largest book fair in 1992. It is now a best seller in the 14th printing with over 100,000 copies sold.

   A.C. Ross' second book _Ehanamani_ _"Walks Among"_ is in the 6th printing. His third book _Keeper of the Female Medicine Bundle_ is in the 4th printing, and _Crazy Horse_ is his 4th book.

   A.C. Ross has lectured on cultural undertanding in 44 states in the U.S., 6 Canadian provinces, 9 European countries and most recently, Japan.